KEN APTEKAR

TALKING TO PICTURES

Introduction by Terrie Sultan

Larger than Life: Reading the Corcoran Collection by Mieke Bal

Aptekar's Family Album by Albert Boime

The Corcoran Gallery of Art, Washington, DC

Published in 1997 by the Corcoran Gallery of Art, 500 Seventeenth Street NW, Washington, DC, 20006, (202) 639–1700.

Sultan, Terrie, 1952 –

Ken Aptekar: talking to pictures / Terrie Sultan, Mieke Bal, Albert Boime.

p. cm.

Catalog of an exhibition to be held at the Corcoran Gallery of Art, Oct. 18, 1997–Feb. 15, 1998.

Includes bibliographical references.

ISBN 088675–053–9

1. Aptekar, Ken, 1950– –Exhibitions. 2. Altered paintings –Exhibitions. I. Aptekar, Ken, 1950– . II, Bal, Mieke. 1946– . III. Boime, Albert. IV. Corcoran Gallery of Art. V. Title.

ND237.A6465A4 1997

759.13–dc21. 97-34488

CIP

KEN APTEKAR: TALKING TO PICTURES

Terrie Sultan, Curator of Contemporary Art

Throughout his career, Ken Aptekar has scrutinized painting from a singular vantage point. Reinterpreting historical paintings in order to encourage viewers to explore their presumptions about the nature of conferred and perceived value, he first creatively repaints details of acknowledged masterworks, and then places glass panels over his painted interpretations; upon these panels are etched narratives that either directly refer to the artworks depicted or express ideas and stories that are associated thematically with the selected images. In Aptekar's work, the conjunction of word and image creates a hybrid discourse that poses elusive questions and forges mysterious connections between what is depicted and what is necessarily left out. Creating an intersection of language and visual image, his work asks us to reevaluate some of our most potent beliefs about the nature of intrinsic, temporal, and conferred value in the aesthetic experience. Like any good story, Aptekar's paintings first confuse and then clarify the attributes of identity. He is well aware of the impact of history on the choices we make and the values we follow. By juxtaposing recognized images with his highly personal narratives, he compresses our long lineage of accumulated knowledge into the pinpoint focus of individual perception, and then uses this sense of individual awareness to bridge the gap between historical presumptions and contemporary thinking.

I first met Ken in 1990, when I invited him to participate in the Corcoran's *43rd Biennial Exhibition of Contemporary American Painting*. His work during that period explored the ideal of maleness; to do this, he juxtaposed painted interpretations of masterworks by Rembrandt and Raphael with biographical and autobiographical texts. As Aptekar continued to mine the territory of representation, figuration, and the intersection of history and the present day, he further distilled his statements about societal and cultural systems of thought. In November 1996 I saw Aptekar's most recent body of work, a series of paintings that even more emphatically intertwined familial biography with historical art. In this series he employed such diverse artists as the relatively unknown nineteenth-century Viennese painter Isidore Kaufmann and the more popularly acknowledged eighteenth-century French court painter François Boucher. A stunning ten-foot square painting, *I'm six years old and hiding behind my hands*, paired the Boucher source painting with an original text that read like a succinct short story. This represented a major leap in both scale and content for Ken. More importantly, it signaled a significant change in the poetry of his narrative language and his technical skills as a painter. His project for the Corcoran is an outgrowth of the ideas initially developed in these paintings.

In *Talking To Pictures*, Aptekar created a series of paintings based specifically on works in the Gallery's collection. Grounded in months of research with the objects and interviews with Corcoran curators, students of the Corcoran School, and museum visitors, this body of work departs from Aptekar's past practice of representing renowned masterworks. Instead, he selected a series of paintings by lesser-known (occasionally unknown) artists from the seventeenth to the early nineteenth century. Over the course of several months, he explored the artworks' subject matter, acquisition and exhibition history, purchase prices, as well as the backgrounds of the original owners and public opinion of each painting. He reviewed hundreds of archival files and spent hours in the permanent collection galleries to complete the preliminary stage of his on-site study. From this initial research, he selected the paintings which comprised the subject matter for the second phase of his project, a series of five discussion groups held with elementary school children, high school students from the School Without Walls, fine arts and critical theory students from the Corcoran School of Art, museum guards, and members of the general public. He posed questions to each group in order to elicit their opinions of the selected paintings, seeking to establish both their aesthetic judgments and their personal responses to the works of art. Combining the results from these discussions with his prior research, Aptekar composed his own narrative texts that form the core of *Talking To Pictures.*

Aptekar's engagement with cultural ideas is greatly enhanced by his knowledge of art, history, and literature in both "high" and "low" cultural formats: he is equally at home with old master paintings and popular forms of music and literature. What he seeks to establish in his paintings is the continuum underlying the disrupted roles and relationships of defined cultural activities and the confusions and intrusions of real life. What he has accomplished in this exhibition is an almost seamless melding of past and present, universal and personal, that makes the process of "talking to pictures" a stimulating and thrilling proposition.

LARGER THAN LIFE: READING THE CORCORAN COLLECTION

Mieke Bal

Ken Aptekar's paintings are defined by two features: they are copies, and they have words on them. Gorgeously painted and visually attractive, they are "simply" copies of old masterpieces. The old masterpiece is wrested from its then-and-there, and planted in the here-and-now. The copy is an after-effect of great painting, belonging to the past and yet available in the present. Once you adjust your expectations and appreciate this postmodern challenge to originality, unreflectively "checking out" the fidelity of the copy, a small, barely perceptible change suddenly and rudely wrenches you out of the past and firmly plants you in the late twentieth century. The emphasis on visuality is broken because the old masterpiece is literally overwritten, overruled by an emphatically autobiographical text. Offering a text that overlays an image, hiding it behind transparent glass, the work's primary effect is an invitation to read.

In *Talking To Pictures* these two defining features converge with a third aspect that highlights the here-and-now of Aptekar's art. He has selected works from the collection of the Corcoran Gallery of Art for his subjects. And, for the first time in his work, Aptekar has made use not only of his own writing but also of viewers' responses to the source paintings. This innovation in his texts reflects the notion that the actual museum situation in which we now view his works is also the institutional setting in which the history of art can be accessed and pressured for a variety of meanings.

It takes an exceedingly long time to read the few lines inscribed over Hobbema's trees in *My parents take us on trips* (PLATE 12):

> *My parents take us on trips. The four kids pile in the car. Often when we're driving, I press my forehead to the window. Sometimes birds perch on telephone wires along the road, and I fly up and sit quietly beside them. They're just there; they have nothing to figure out, no one to escape.*

As a viewer, I step into this childhood world, become the little boy, fly up with him to sit next to the birds. For I, too, spent many boring hours thinking, figuring out the mysteries of life, escaping from the cruelty of other children, the bossiness of well-meaning parents, the increasing sense of powerlessness. The work's intimacy challenges everything we think we know about the difference between visual and verbal domains. Aptekar's painting challenges the common assumptions that these media are different, but it also questions *how* they differ. *My parents take*

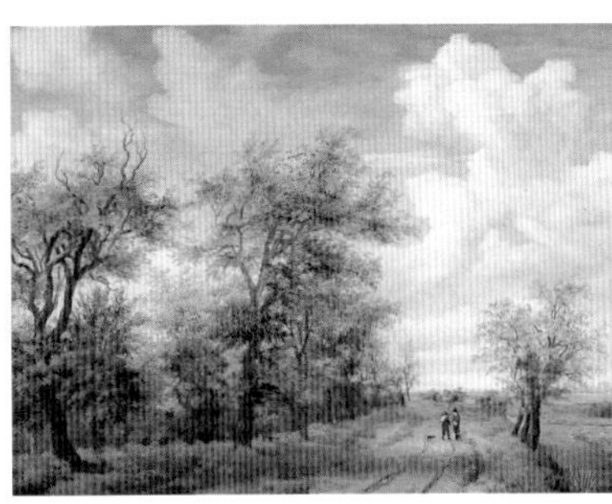

Meyndert Hobbema
A Wooded Landscape with Figures, c. 1663

us on trips contains a tiny element that connects visual and verbal, past to present: the birds on the telephone wire that Aptekar has inserted into his copy of Hobbema's *Wooded Landscape with Figures* link Aptekar to Hobbema, child to adult. The birds stand for the world outside the subject. But one of them is the child; didn't he just say that he flew up to sit quietly beside them? The child flew up from the text into the image. Flying up, fantasizing, is the child's primary means of escape. The glass plate overlayering the painting suggests the car window, the anachronistic window-on-the-world that painting cannot be, but can appear to be as we are taken in by a persuasive fiction.

Talking To Pictures, the title of this exhibition, suggests many meanings, from the literal quotation of audience responses, to the words addressing the images from their proximate but separate layer of glass, to the child flying up to sit in the picture, to the people here and now, walking through the room of the Corcoran to talk about Aptekar's paintings. Any visual or textual expression is a patchwork of fragments taken from different sources. The fragments have a memory. At the same time, every reuse of preexisting material changes it. The telephone wire carries Hobbema along with it, the long tradition of landscape painting, the competition between human effort and nature that is larger than life. No wonder that, in the journey from past to present, Aptekar's representation of Hobbema has doubled in size.

Compare *My parents take us on trips* with *It wasn't my brother who shot the rabbi* (PLATE 13). The portrait by Charles Loring Elliott from 1856 stands firmly in the tradition of portraiture, which is defined by its ability to bestow authority upon its subject. Its history is bound up with that of capitalism, individualism, and bourgeois culture. This somewhat pompous portrait from the Corcoran collection fits the bill perfectly. The sitter's chin expresses self-assurance, the eyes look at us from a seat of power that resides deep within the soul. The frame, even more pompous than the painting, confirms what the genre implies: portraits are made to honor power. But Aptekar cannot be trusted. Even as he faithfully copies it, he pokes fun at the authority that inheres in portraiture. He reverses the painting, making it slightly darker by toning it brown, as if it has faded with time, depriving the frame of its golden luster and decorative pomp. Through the artist's barely perceptible interventions, the sitter's gaze has turned inward, casting doubt on the certainty and self-confidence that the sitter originally expressed in Elliott's painting.

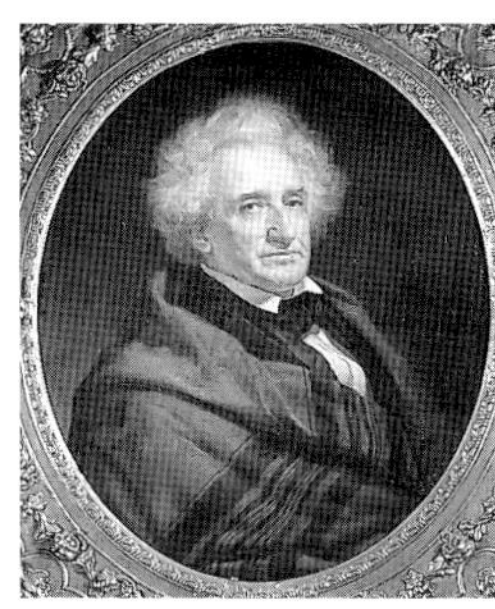

Charles Loring Elliott
Thomas Loraine McKenney, 1856

Furthermore, the frame is cropped, the painting pushed to one side. The authority figure is still present, but he has become stilted, so to speak. Rendering the eyes of authority in the original into those of hurt and anxiety in the copy, Aptekar endows the bourgeois power broker with the hint of a history that makes him more human and understandable. The eyes, like the telephone wire, are an intervention that hinges different genres, worlds, and times.

Set to the lower left of the painted portrait, the text appears contiguous with the sitter, as if it could be coming out of his mouth, if only his mouth were not so firmly closed.

> *It wasn't my brother who shot the rabbi to death before a packed synagogue in a wealthy suburb of Detroit. The killer was some other kid's mentally ill older brother. He strode up to the front of the sanctuary on a spring day in 1966, and announced over the mike, "This synagogue is an abomination and a travesty," then faced Rabbi Morris Adler and pulled out his gun. The beloved rabbi fell to the floor, his prayer shawl still draped around him. The boy turned the gun on himself, and a family secret became a public tragedy.*

Irresistibly, the prayer shawl—the moving detail that connects the deceased private person with the public function for which he was killed—rhymes with the blanket draped around the man in the picture. Information in the Corcoran archives tells us that the sitter was a Commissioner of Indian Affairs, who apparently received this blanket from his constituents as a symbol of respect.

From many of the works in this exhibition the visitor learns that Aptekar is Jewish and that this identity is inextricably knotted into his subjectivity. So, it *could have been* his older brother. One kid, another kid, a tragedy in a synagogue. Tragedy: the oldest literary genre in Western culture, from the Greeks, who staged the overwhelming power of the gods, destiny, and history over human heroism and goodness. Tragedy: the genre beyond good and evil, human-sized morality, individual effort. The autobiographical, understated, very short stories that Aptekar writes over his paintings become larger than life through this bold appropriation of this most prestigious of literary genres. Thus, the emptiness of public authority is filled with the private grief of the eyes. This painting's critique of institutional and familial authority diagnoses our culture but does not lay blame. Although Aptekar takes the portrait genre to task for allowing itself to become a cultural instrument, he does not, as one might expect, deindividualize the sitter. His very act of painting, of copying, asserts his awareness that you cannot reject painting and continue to paint.

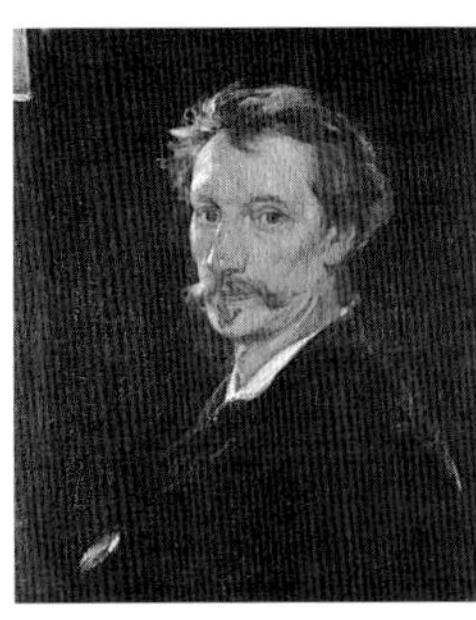

Walter Shirlaw
Self–Portrait, n.d.

Aptekar challenges an image's authority in three ways. First, he inserts a sense of time through the tiny changes he makes in what initially appear to be "faithful" copies. More strongly, he makes our gaze stumble or fall over his words, which slow us down, and by forcing us to slow down, stimulates the act of looking. Finally, the competition between text and image enforces a backtracking and moving forward; occluding our sense of purpose from start to finish, this shifting focus reinforces our "being" in time. From the rabbi's prayer shawl we move back to the portrayed man's blanket, and are trapped in questions of identity in relation to power. Forced to compare the rabbi's own prayer shawl with the sitter's blanket, given to him by the Indians he represented, we cannot help noticing the sitter's use of the blanket to demonstrate his definitive position of power. By enforcing the constant interruption of one medium with another, Aptekar's art simultaneously acknowledges and challenges our preoccupation with the fixity of the visual image. He ties the experience of looking to an awareness of looking-and-reading in "real" time. The problem of "memory" and the perpetual transformation of signs and meanings lies in the tension between the power of the present social world—for Aptekar, this includes his family as well as institutions—and the past, which keeps creeping in yet eludes any attempt to grasp it firmly.

Faith, being, reality, and memory are central to many of the works in this exhibition. In "*Is that you?*" (PLATE 16), Walter Shirlaw's self-portrait is pulled forward, made greener, and overwritten with the casual remark of an art student, one of the people whom Aptekar invited to "talk to these pictures."

> *"Is that you?" the art student asks. I tell him it's a self-portrait by Walter Shirlaw from around 1880. The art student tells me to forget about the Shirlaw. "Boring," he says.*

The text takes us away from the intimacy of autobiography, toward the casual, not-so-profound conversation between artist and art student, from tragedy and deep emotion to babble and boredom. But look what happens in the process. Aptekar's version of Shirlaw's portrait does look like the artist. The closed lips refuse to talk; the eyes are squarely turned toward the viewer yet refuse to specify an expression; intense yet still, they peer out yet appear also to stare inward. The greenish, pale complexion, the shade of hair, all suggest a redhead. The face comes forward to fill more of the picture, the contrived pose of the bust has been cropped away. And whereas the

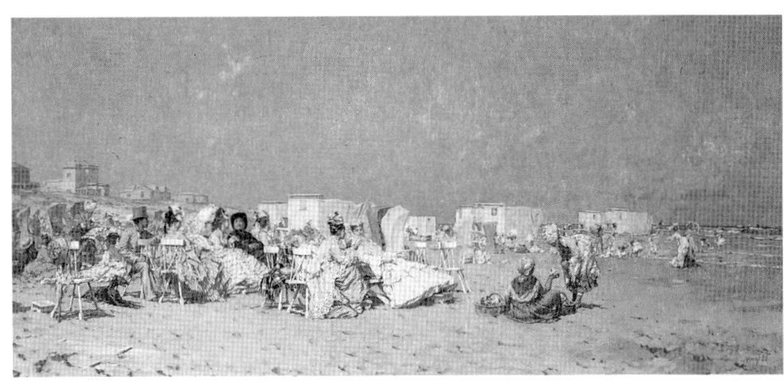

Frederick Hendrick Kaemmerer
The Beach at Scheveningen, Holland, 1874

autobiographical text yields to the second person, emphasized both by the use of "you" and by the question, Aptekar literally pushes the sitter forward. The self-portrait is the painted image's version of autobiography. But Aptekar's polemic against individualism in *It wasn't my brother who shot the rabbi* lingers. Through the temporal displacement between "I" and "you," the self-portrait of another becomes an "other," or alternate, portrait of the self.

What is this eerie resemblance between Aptekar and another man's self-portrait? The sensitivity in the face is kept at bay in the Shirlaw through a traditional pose that creates a double distance. "Boring" is the word that gives voice to these subtle features. Again, the art student was right. But when he dismissed the spatial distancing that is part of Shirlaw's history, he had not yet seen what Aptekar did to the traditional work. The contemporary artist understands more of the distant figure, and pulls him closer, literally toward the proximity of a close-up. Once more, Aptekar questions individualism by means of a subtle, inclusive gesture. "*Is that you?*" draws attention to a rarely used genre of narrative which is often perceived as artificial or experimental—narrative in the second person. In painting, this technique is embodied as a shift in the sitter's frontality. This self/other portrait conveys narrative visually through the slight turning of the head in relation to the body, but this is a narrative that, while it happens in the here-and-now, is described in the second person. Did the sitter hear the student ask the question "Is that you?" so that he could not help but respond? Our acknowledgment, or presumption of the viewer as speaker is the key to interpreting this work. In the process, the art student's casual and discontinuous remarks have suddenly lost their superficiality.

Portraiture and self-portraiture, made more complex through temporal delay and exchange between artist and subject, self and other, establish one of Aptekar's persistent themes. Several of the works in this exhibition explicitly address issues of identity; most of them also refer to it implicitly. The very first painting, an empty frame, is a good case of the latter. The frame, especially since it opens the show, functions like a poetic invocation about the art we are about to see. By placing the empty frame of a "ghost painting" at the beginning of his show, the artist encourages the audience to reframe other paintings. The summery blue skies of the beach scene in the next painting—connected to this one by reuse of the same frame—set the tone in coloristic terms: blue and gold. The blue is a bit muted, evoking a hazy summer day. But what does

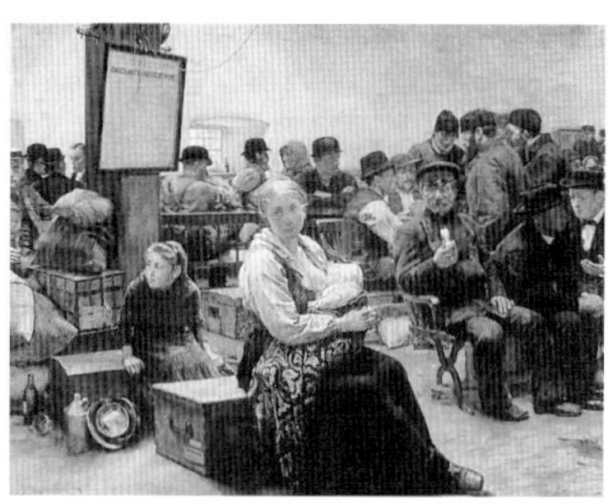

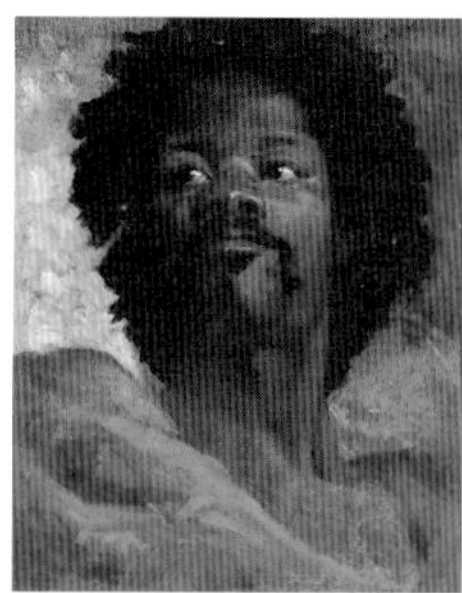

Charles Frederick Ulrich,
In the Land of Promise, Castle Garden, 1884

Henri Regnault,
Head of a Moor, 1870

the frame do, framing nothing? Well, it's not quite true that it frames nothing. For what is inside the frame may be the same as what is outside of it—just blue, devoid of figures, but referring to a particular kind of summer day. And the frame is not arbitrary. Leaving its shadow both inside itself, at the upper border, and outside itself, below, it asserts the work of framing as the essence of Aptekar's aesthetic.

The second painting (PLATE 2), based on a merry beach scene from 1874 by Frederick Hendrick Kaemmerer (now deaccessioned), is overwritten by Aptekar's childhood memories of summer. Into this nostalgia Aptekar inserts a fragment of the empty frame, emphasizing the act of framing as an act of isolation and aggrandizement. The section of the reversed Kaemmerer that is isolated within the golden frame (and made slightly darker, so as to look less faded, more present) does not represent the closer bourgeois ladies, but the merchant woman sitting at a subtly isolating distance. Dressed in poorer clothes, her skin is browner than that of the lady to whom she is offering her merchandise. This picturesque detail, that makes the original painting more lively, and the scene more revealing of past social mores, is represented by Aptekar to show fragments of modern life as it was, then.

Aptekar isolates the merchant woman doubly; putting her inside the frame and moving her higher, to the left. The social structure within this innocent summer scene has now been reframed to emphasize the one woman who is different from the others. Brown-skinned, faced with the imperative of making a living instead of the consumption of leisure, she is, in Kaemmerer's painting, an isolated object of curiosity, or neglect. She does not benefit from the admiring gaze of the man who appears to be sitting, waiting to take his pick. Here, too, Aptekar writes himself into the frame. Like the ladies, he always had to wear clothes at the beach. In his case, this was not due to social convention, but because of the sensitivity of his lightly colored skin.

This narratively reduced figure is evoked again later in the show in *I went searching for Jews* (PLATE 9). Unlike Aptekar's other paintings, which infer, this painting explicitly links past to present, other to self. "Russian Jews, like me," he says. He found them in an 1884 painting of an immigration landing depot by Charles Frederick Ulrich. Aptekar's reworked painting is saved from irremediable sentimentality by the authority of the gazes and the arbitrary cropping of the scene. Aptekar is quite specific here: "I found them in the background, huddled, anxious, busy."

At this point, resonances begin to fill the room, and the paintings seem to be talking to one another. The self-portrait after Shirlaw, projecting the individual into the foreground, jostles with the woman at the beach, who has been lifted out of the background, but not to the close-up of individual portraiture.

Henri Regnault's 1870 portrait of a black man, beautiful as it is, is not based on any such spatial dislocation. It is not unsympathetic; its portrait perspective, with the artist viewing the sitter from below, makes the figure look heroic. But the way color is used emphasizes blackness, so that it can only be seen as the opposite of identification. This is done not only by the facial color itself, which is black as black people rarely are, setting off the whites of the eye, but also by the bright yellow on the left, and by the deep crimson garment. Aptekar uses this painting twice, as if to compensate for the scarcity of black subjects in the Corcoran's collection.

Aptekar has reversed this portrait (PLATE 10); he has also cropped the bright colors, and kept only the most essential part of the face. Most importantly, the painting has become monochromatic, to avoid the picturesque coloring of the original. When painted in one color, the face regains its nuances, and the visibility that was taken away by excessive darkness is reinstated. The text written over this painting is neither long nor narrative. It endows the features of the face with positive feedback, and it connects audience to figure through an explicit identification that is based not on skin color but on individual features of identity. As the symmetrical counterpart to the authoritative yet sad sitter in *It wasn't my brother who shot the rabbi*, this figure is retrospectively accorded the "Strength. Determination. Power." that Regnault, by overloading his color sense and rendering his facial features invisible, denied. Carrie Parker, young, female, contemporary, endows the figure with these positive features as much as she takes them from him for her own benefit: "And that's a little like myself" is her conclusion.

Identification is also the basis of the other portrait after this Regnault (PLATE 14), which appears in this exhibition after *It wasn't my brother who shot the rabbi*. Here, the burnt umber of *Strength. Determination. Power.* has been replaced with an overall blue that denaturalizes color altogether. This effect is emphasized by the addition of a frame. The story Aptekar tells is about a Jewish boy delving into black culture. The thrill of transgressing is audible—"I tried to be cool"—and the pride the boy felt when his older brother managed to participate in "the best of the be-bop

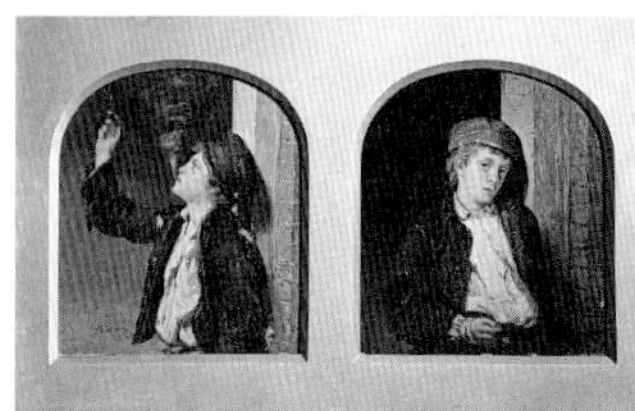

John George Brown
Allegro, 1864; and *Penseroso,* 1865

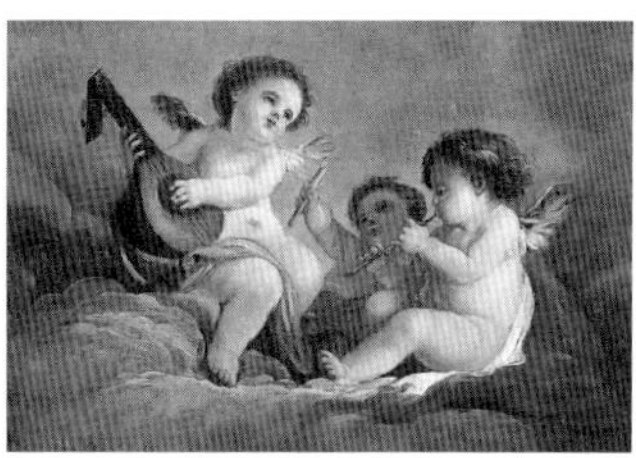

Jean Mari Dedeban
Harpsichord (cupid groupings on the side), 1770

bands" conveys the past "feel" of the story, more than it does the simple declarative of the past tense. The musical phrase "the best of the be-bop bands," with its alliteration and short drumming words, leaves an echo of be-bop as if we had been there too. This is identity poetics, not politics. This memory puts the autobiographical subject on the threshold of adulthood, on the threshold of a culture at a time of *de facto* segregation, on the threshold, again, where self and other meet. In any case, the threshold is marked by the frame, which can be seen as a boundary that keeps distinctions in place, or a meeting point where a greeting yields to an embrace.

I have tried, using a number of examples, to suggest how Aptekar has worked to make paintings that move beyond identity politics into the carefully probed realm of potential harmony. As the artist wrote in *When he was twenty* (PLATE 19), "I find myself drawn now to scenes of harmony." This harmony is not sentimental or idealist. Rather, the interpenetration of private and public life, of institutional pressures and familial tragedy, overwrites the rococo sentimentality of gentile cuteness, painted as if to conjure up and then excise what cannot be. To be or not to be: Shakespeare's question of identity is both omnipresent and relativized throughout this installation. Aptekar explores tenaciously yet makes his labors appear easy. As fourteen-year-old Akosua Tyus says in *I know there's lots of kids smoking* (PLATE 23): "But art is art, and all art doesn't send a positive message."

"Good" messages are not always available; often, they are deceptively simple. Aptekar has also introduced a lot of unsettling, worrying, and anxiety-inducing messages here. One way or another, both positive and negative messages relate to the way an individual's voice is erased or undermined by authority, both within the family and within institutions. The diagnosis is sharp, and the analogy between family and institution is inexact, but Aptekar's view is always compassionate instead of complaining. Critical analysis, yes, razor-sharp. But there are no "bad" messages. Aptekar takes us through a body of painting in order to make us think of ourselves. The interaction between public institutional pressures and the private life of the viewer always comes back to haunt public culture: in Aptekar's work, this interaction is scrutinized and projected literally into the space of the viewer. This sense of empowerment makes us all, if only for a short time, larger than life.

The curator refers to ghosts in the collection. She's smiling, but she's not happy. I'm puzzled. "Paintings the museum sold off," she explains.

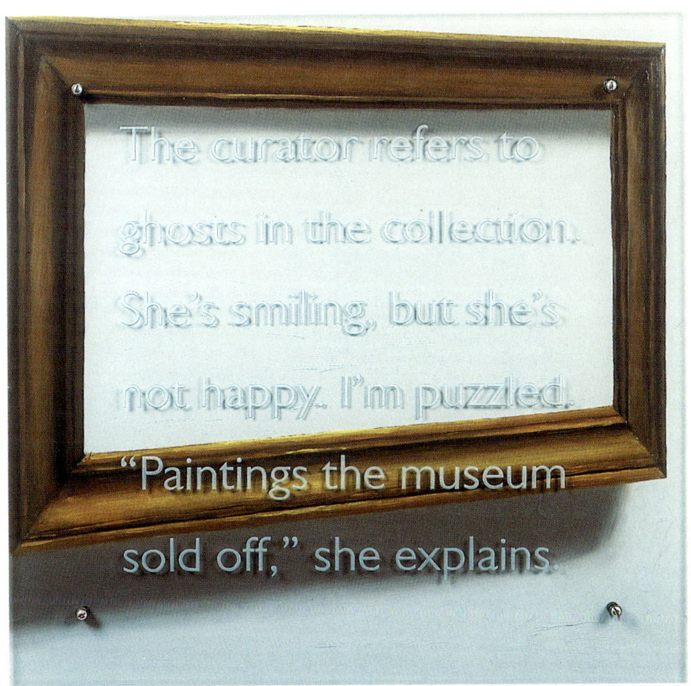

PLATE I

The curator refers to ghosts, 1997
Oil on wood, bolts, sandblasted glass
30" x 30"
Courtesy of Jack Shainman Gallery, New York

Summers we drive up to East Tawas on Lake Huron. There the sky is much bigger than over the backyard in Detroit. The sun is hotter, too. Even in the water I have to wear a t-shirt. Lying on the sand I watch rabbits and mushrooms drift across the sky. I am the baby, and they love me: Mom, Dad, my sister, my two big brothers. They don't have to cover up. They're not redheads.

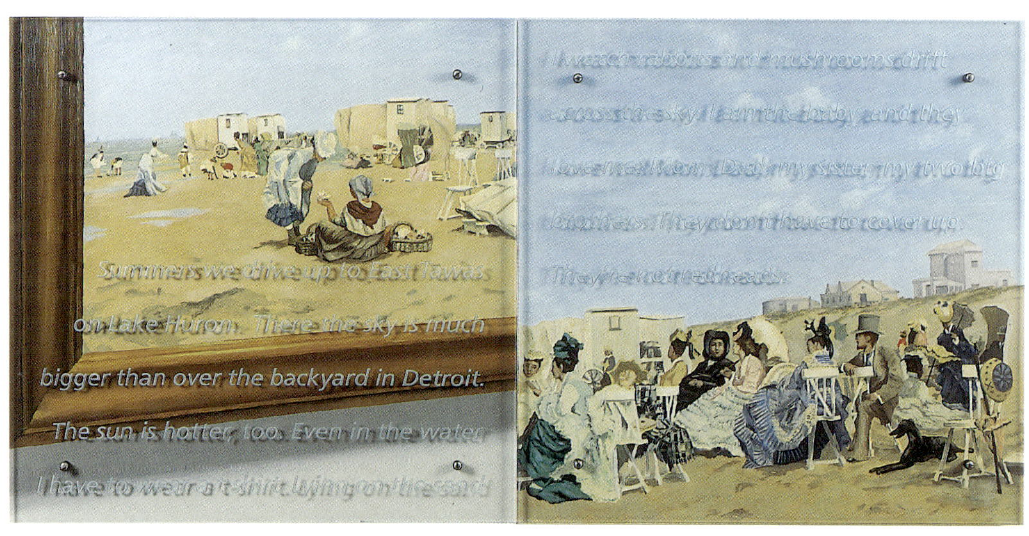

PLATE 2

Summers we drive up to East Tawas, 1997
Oil on wood, bolts, sandblasted glass
30" x 60" (2 panels)
Courtesy of Jack Shainman Gallery, New York

Bruce Holmes, 14: If he wanted to be feminine, that's him. I wouldn't deprive him of that. For me personally, it's like, whatever floats your boat.

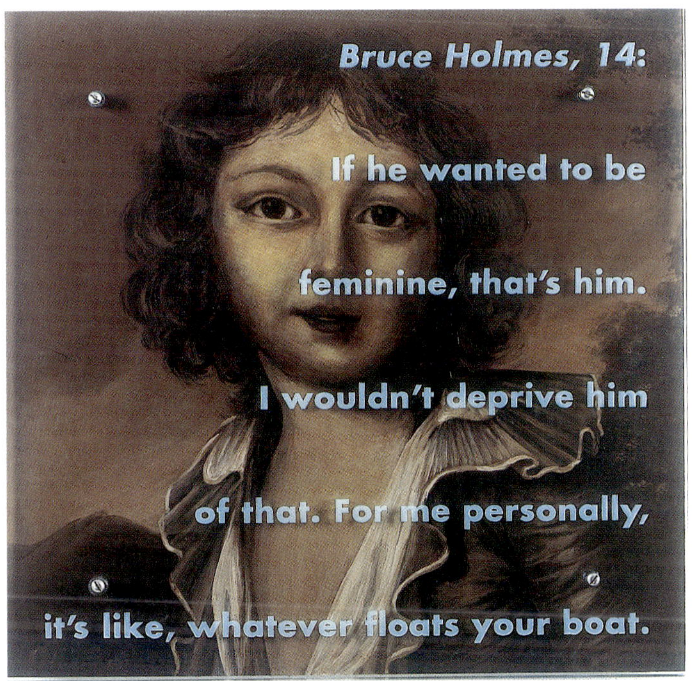

PLATE 3

If he wanted to be feminine, 1997
Oil on wood, bolts, sandblasted glass
24" x 24"
Courtesy of Jack Shainman Gallery, New York

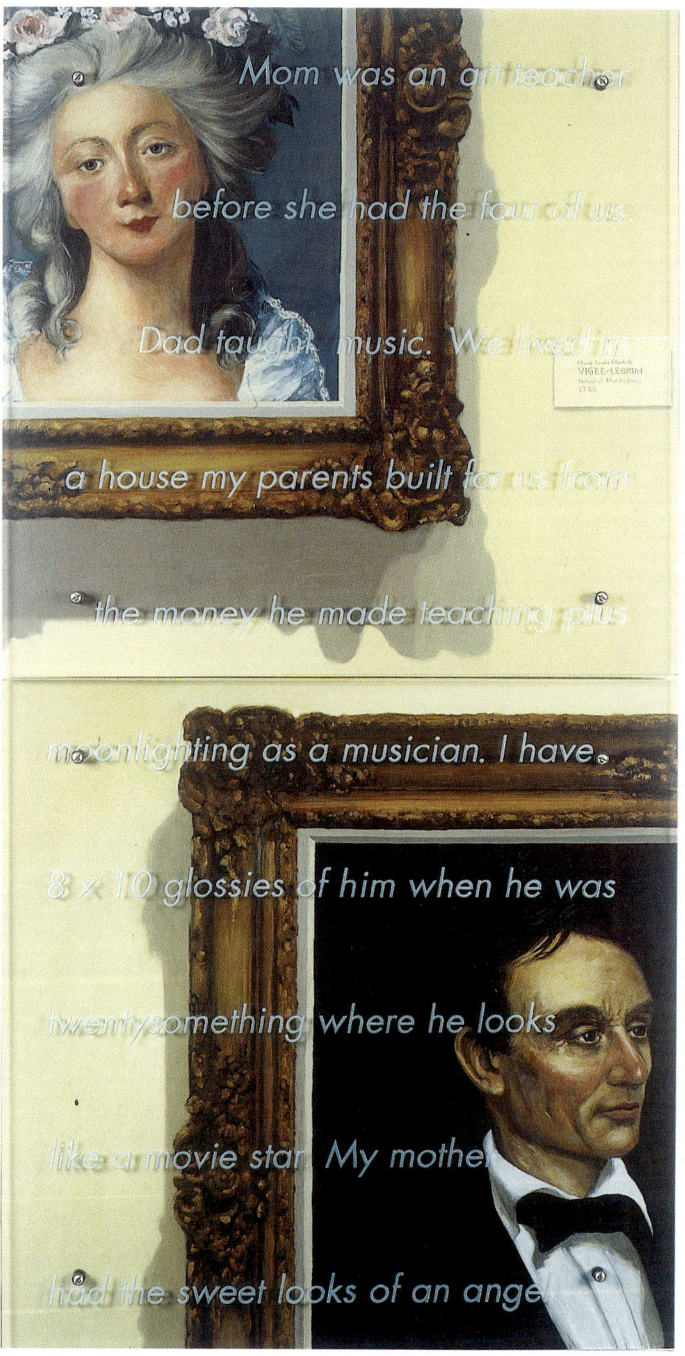

Mom was an art teacher, before she had the four of us. Dad taught music. We lived in a house my parents built for us from the money he made teaching plus moonlighting as a musician. I have 8 x 10 glossies of him when he was twentysomething where he looks like a movie star. My mother had the sweet looks of an angel.

PLATE 4

Mom was an art teacher, 1997
Oil on wood, bolts,
sandblasted glass
60" x 30" (2 panels)
Collection of Cynthia Stein

Her father dragged her from shtetl to shtetl. She sewed clothes for Jews in the back of a horse-drawn cart. A marriage to an older man was arranged but Mierle Pomerance escaped. Uncle Shmulik secretly arranged passage, and alone she sailed to America. Stepping off the train in Detroit, she found a job in two days. Two weeks later Mierle, now Mary, had a boyfriend; and when the relatives she stayed with disapproved, she got herself a room. They wed in her landlord's apartment and feasted on corned beef sandwiches. She managed the bicycle shop they ran; he shmoozed with customers. Still she found the time to make my mother's clothes: a red and white gingham outfit, a pink suit with a blue organdy blouse. "A couturière your grandma could've been!" my mother says. I escaped when I became an artist.

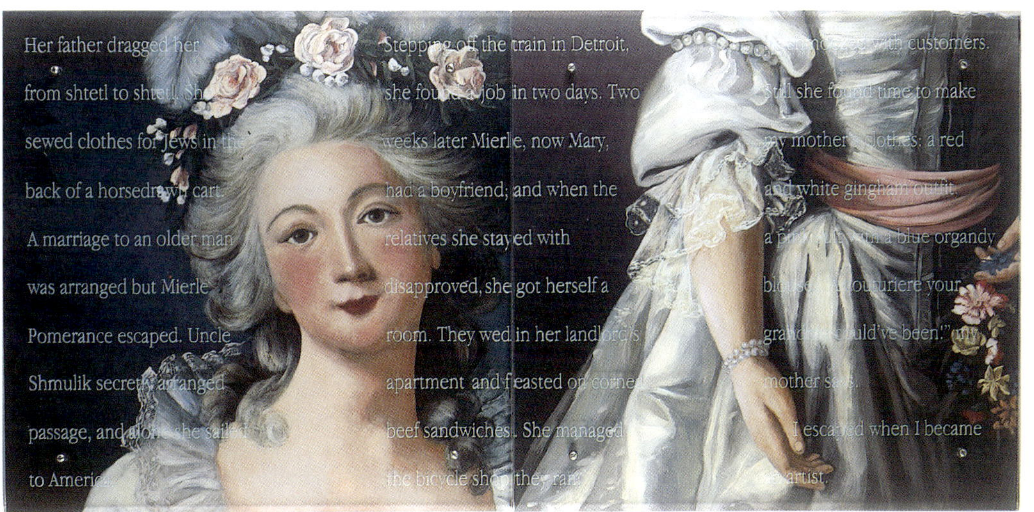

PLATE 5

"A couturière your grandma could've been!," 1997
Oil on wood, bolts, sandblasted glass
30" x 60" (2 panels)
Collection of Marcia Cohn Spiegel

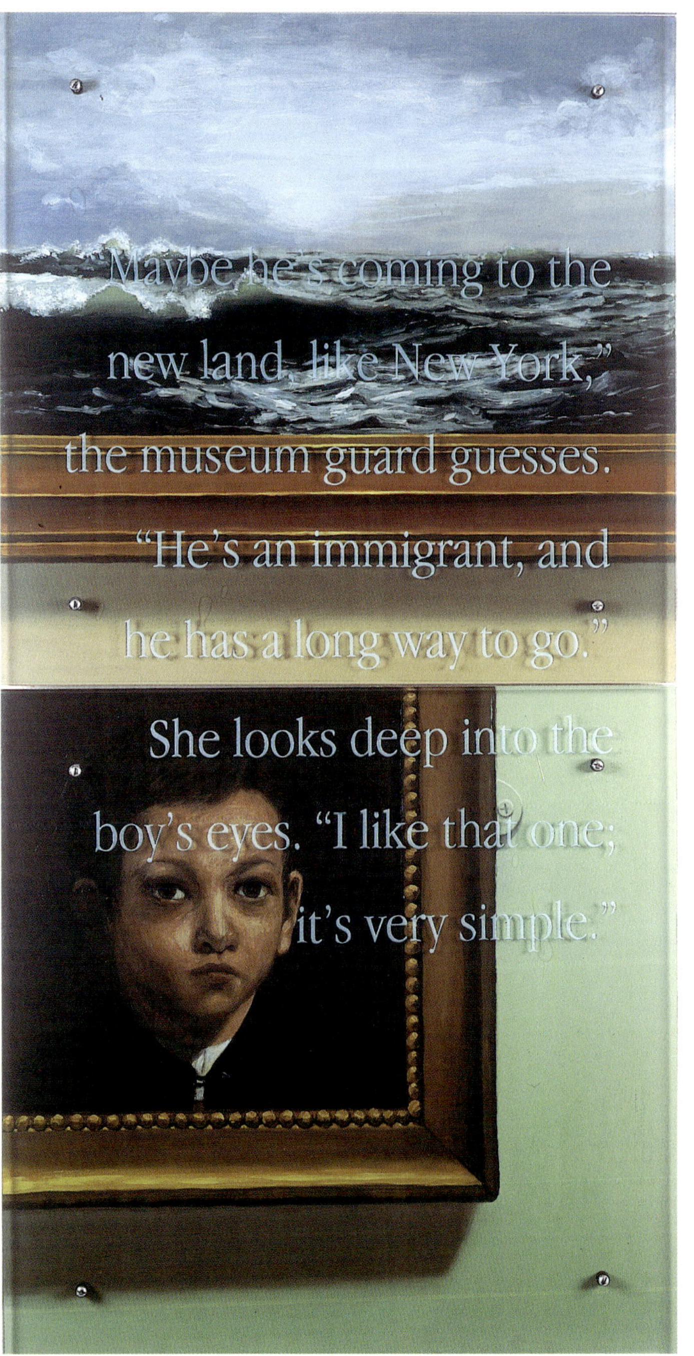

"Maybe he's coming to the new land, like New York," the museum guard guesses. "He's an immigrant, and he has a long way to go." She looks deep into the boy's eyes. "I like that one; it's very simple."

PLATE 6

"Maybe he's coming to the new land,"
1997
Oil on wood, bolts, sandblasted glass
60" x 30" (2 panels)
Collection of Drs. Ernest and Louise De Salvo

Why couldn't you be something better than an artist, Liliana Martin-del-Campo thinks they're saying. She's in the sixth grade. "They're worried their son isn't making any money," she tells me, "and they volunteered to pose for him so he could paint a picture. But they really wanted him to be something like his father was." She doesn't know his father was an artist.

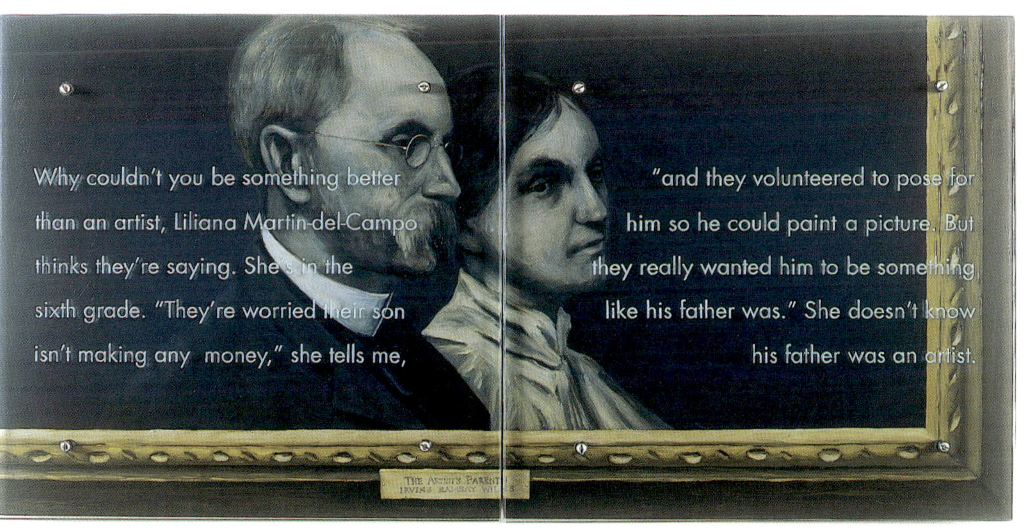

PLATE 7

Why couldn't you be something better than an artist, 1997
Oil on wood, bolts, sandblasted glass
24" x 48" (2 panels)
Courtesy of Jack Shainman Gallery, New York

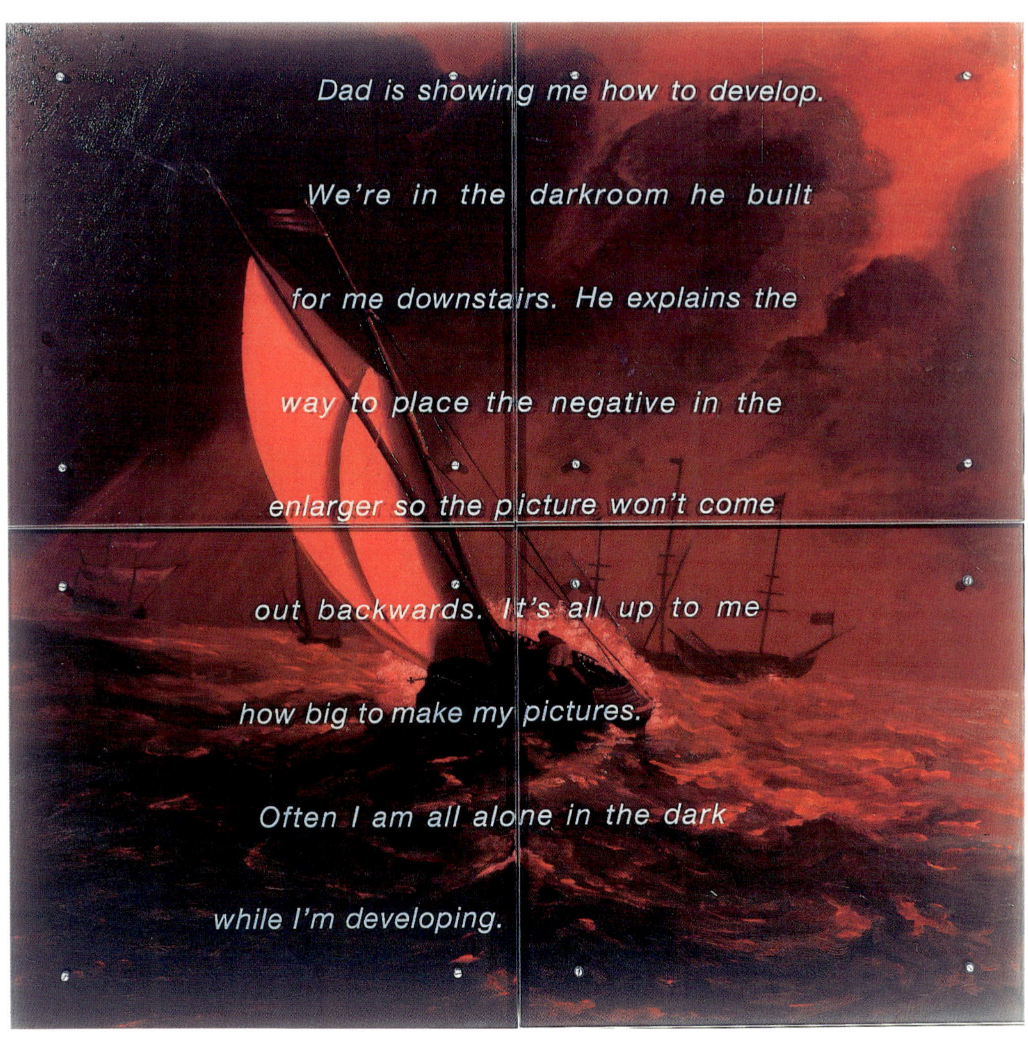

PLATE 8

Dad is showing me how to develop, 1997
Oil on wood, bolts, sandblasted glass
60" x 60" (4 panels)
Courtesy of Jack Shainman Gallery, New York

Dad is showing me how to develop. We're in the darkroom he built for me downstairs. He explains the way to place the negative in the enlarger so the picture won't come out backwards. It's all up to me how big to make my pictures. Often I am all alone in the dark while I'm developing.

I went searching for Jews in the Corcoran. Russian Jews, like me. I found them in the background, huddled, anxious, busy.

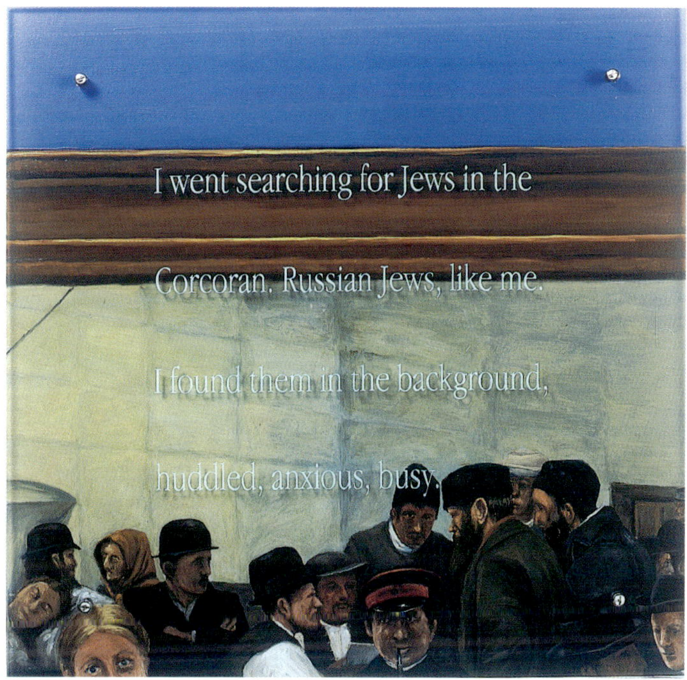

PLATE 9

I went searching for Jews, 1997
Oil on wood, bolts, sandblasted glass
30" x 30"
Collection of Dr. Gail Postal

Strength. Determination. Power. And that's a little like myself. Carrie Parker, age 15

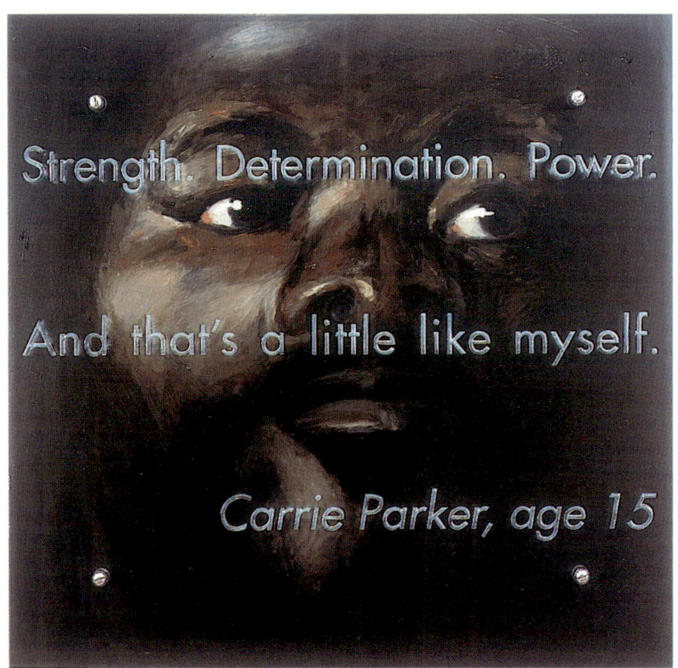

PLATE 10

Strength. Determination. Power., 1997
Oil on wood, bolts, sandblasted glass
24" x 24"
Collection of Dr. Lucy Daniels Inman

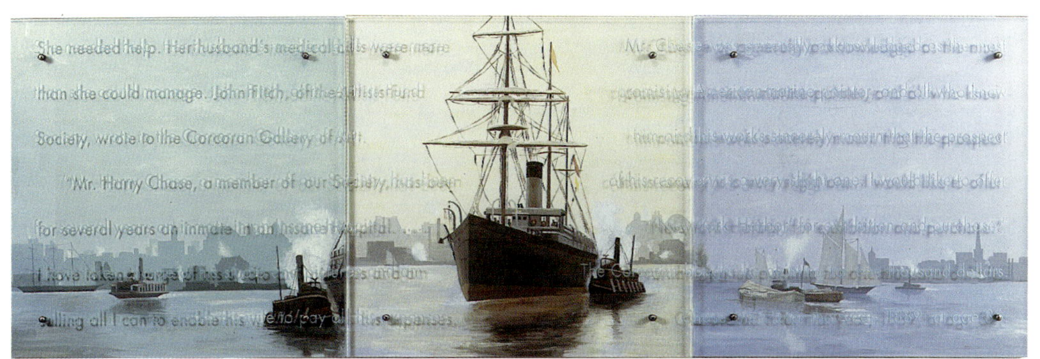

She needed help. Her husband's medical bills were more than she could manage. John Fitch, of the Artists Fund Society, wrote to the Corcoran Gallery of Art. "Mr. Harry Chase, a member of our Society, has been for several years an inmate in an Insane Hospital.... I have taken charge of his studio and pictures and am selling all I can to enable his wife to pay all his expenses. Mr. Chase was generally acknowledged as the most promising American marine painter, and all who knew him and his works sincerely mourn that the prospect of his recovery is a very slight one. I would like to offer 'New York Harbor' for exhibition and purchase." The Corcoran bought the painting for one thousand dollars. Chase died later that year, 1889, at age 36.

PLATE 11

She needed help, 1997
Oil on wood, bolts, sandblasted glass
30" x 90" (3 panels)
Courtesy of Jack Shainman Gallery, New York

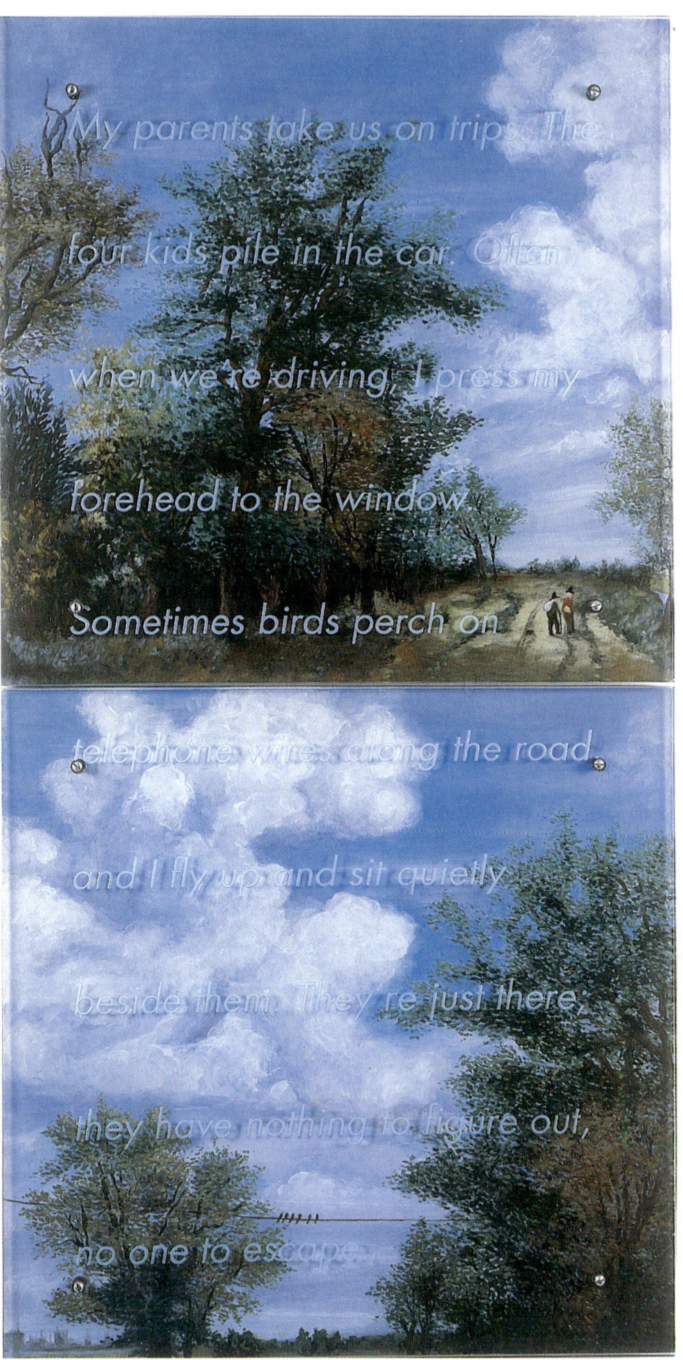

My parents take us on trips. The four kids pile in the car. Often when we're driving, I press my forehead to the window. Sometimes birds perch on telephone wires along the road, and I fly up and sit quietly beside them. They're just there; they have nothing to figure out, no one to escape.

PLATE 12

My parents take us on trips, 1997
Oil on wood, bolts,
sandblasted glass
60" x 30" (2 panels)
Collection of
Dr. Lucy Daniels Inman

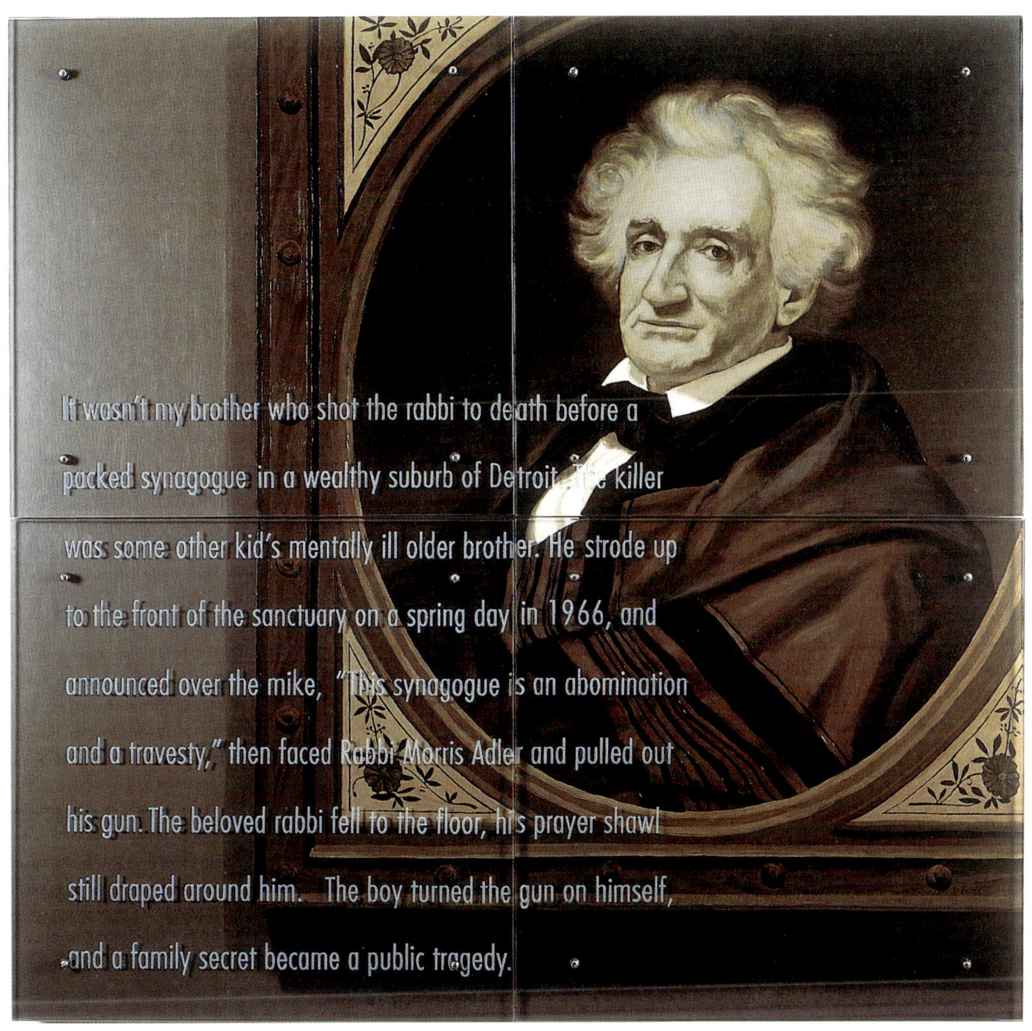

It wasn't my brother who shot the rabbi to death before a packed synagogue in a wealthy suburb of Detroit. The killer was some other kid's mentally ill older brother. He strode up to the front of the sanctuary on that spring day in 1966, and announced over the mike, "This synagogue is an abomination and a travesty," then faced Rabbi Morris Adler and pulled out his gun. The beloved rabbi fell to the floor, his prayer shawl still draped around him. The boy turned the gun on himself, and a family secret became a public tragedy.

PLATE 13

It wasn't my brother who shot the rabbi, 1997
Oil on wood, bolts, sandblasted glass
60" x 60" (4 panels)
Courtesy of Jack Shainman Gallery, New York

After his license was suspended, I drove my older brother to bars in Detroit where whites didn't go. I tried to be cool, sitting down in a booth with my ginger ale. My brother unzipped his gig bag, raised his trumpet, and sat in with the best of the be-bop bands.

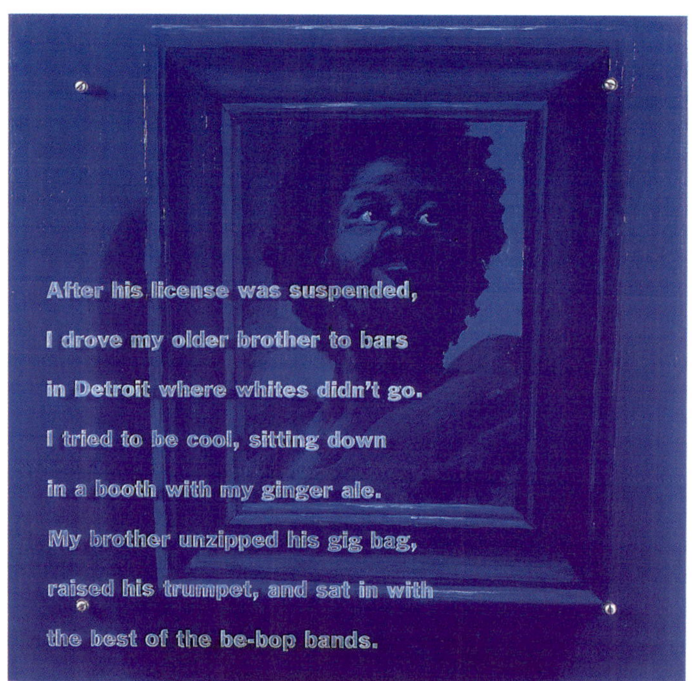

PLATE 14

After his license was suspended, 1997
Oil on wood, bolts, sandblasted glass
30" x 30"
Collection of Ron and Anne Dees

Is the sky blue? What kind of blue? Would I think twice about the clouds? I can't tell from a photograph of the painting. Sotheby's refuses to tell me who bought the beach scene they auctioned for the Corcoran in 1988. They won't even forward my letter asking if I can take a look. The winning bid was $1.2 million. The $122,500 commission the buyer paid Sotheby's bought protection from inquiring artists.

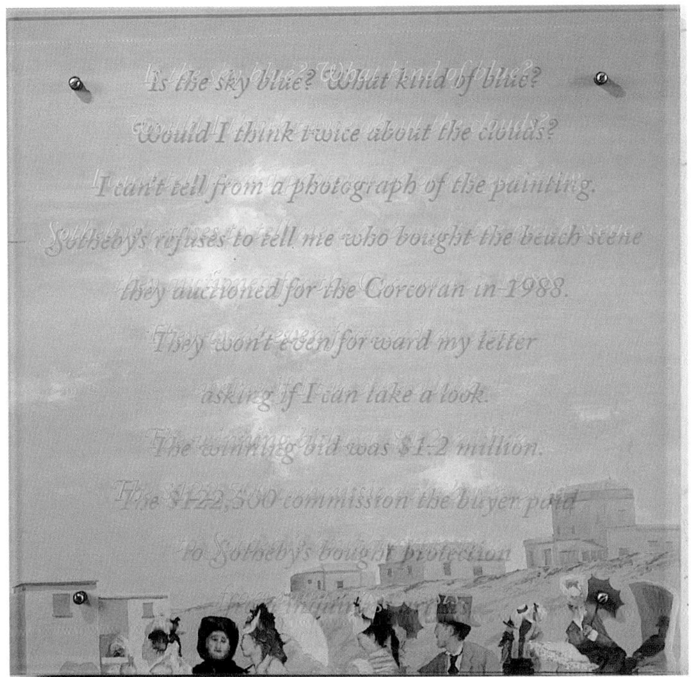

PLATE 15

Is the sky blue?, 1997
Oil on wood, bolts, sandblasted glass
30" x 30"
Courtesy of Jack Shainman Gallery, New York

"Is that you?" the art student asks. I tell him it's a self-portrait by Walter Shirlaw from around 1880. The art student tells me to forget about the Shirlaw. "Boring," he says.

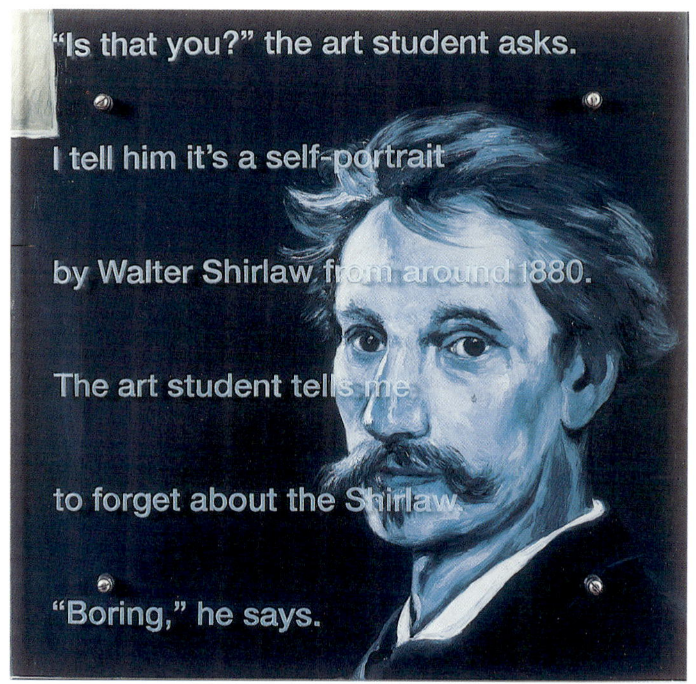

PLATE 16

"Is that you?," 1997
Oil on wood, bolts, sandblasted glass
24" x 24"
Private collection

I'm practicing. Dad's in the other room, but I know he is listening. He cares about how I play the piano. Later my Russian grandmother is sitting on the couch. I'm playing Oyfn Pripetshik for her. I see her lips moving to the Yiddish lyrics she learned in a village near Minsk sixty years ago. My grandma died in 1982. I don't play piano much anymore.

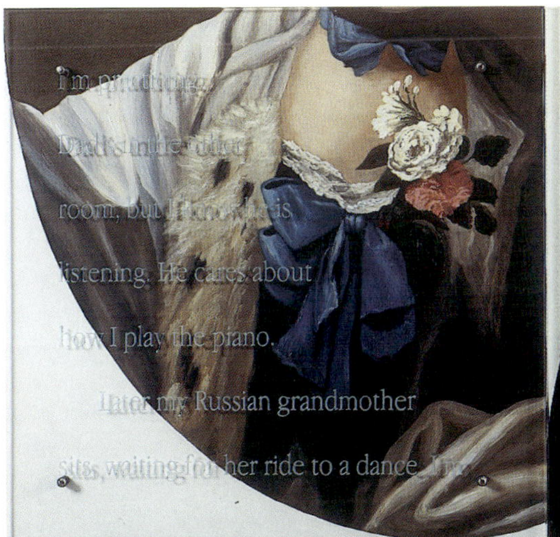

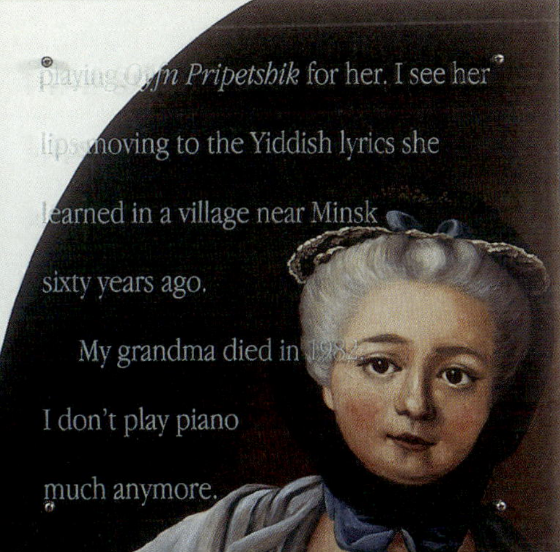

PLATE 17

I'm practicing, 1997
Oil on wood, bolts, sandblasted glass
30" x 60" (2 panels)
Courtesy of Jack Shainman Gallery, New York

I don't like anything about the room in the painting. If I were in it, I'd be wondering where am I supposed to go? I don't want to sit on the chairs, they're uncomfortable. I don't like the colors, they're bland. And I don't like the pots, the little sculpture things. I don't like the picture. You're just focusing on everything that's in the picture, not the picture. Maia Stern, age 11.

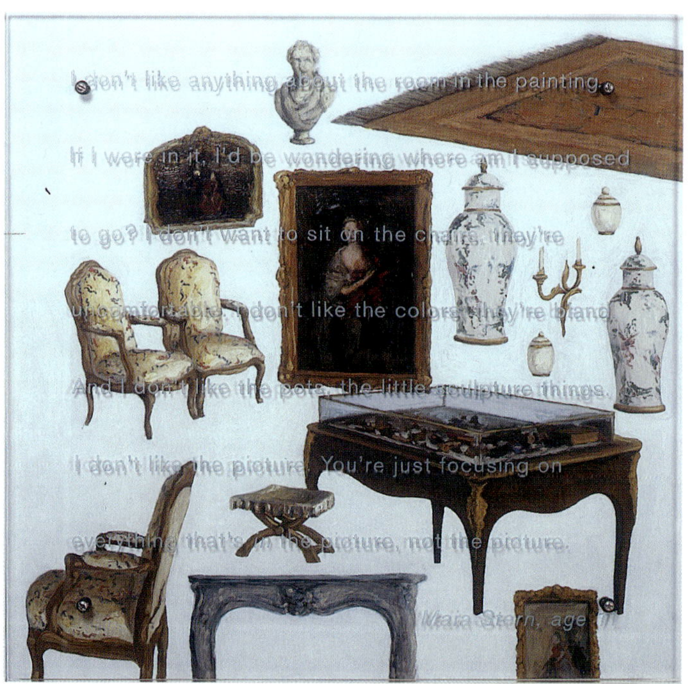

PLATE 18

I don't like anything about the room, 1997
Oil on wood, bolts, sandblasted glass
30" x 30"
Courtesy of Jack Shainman Gallery, New York

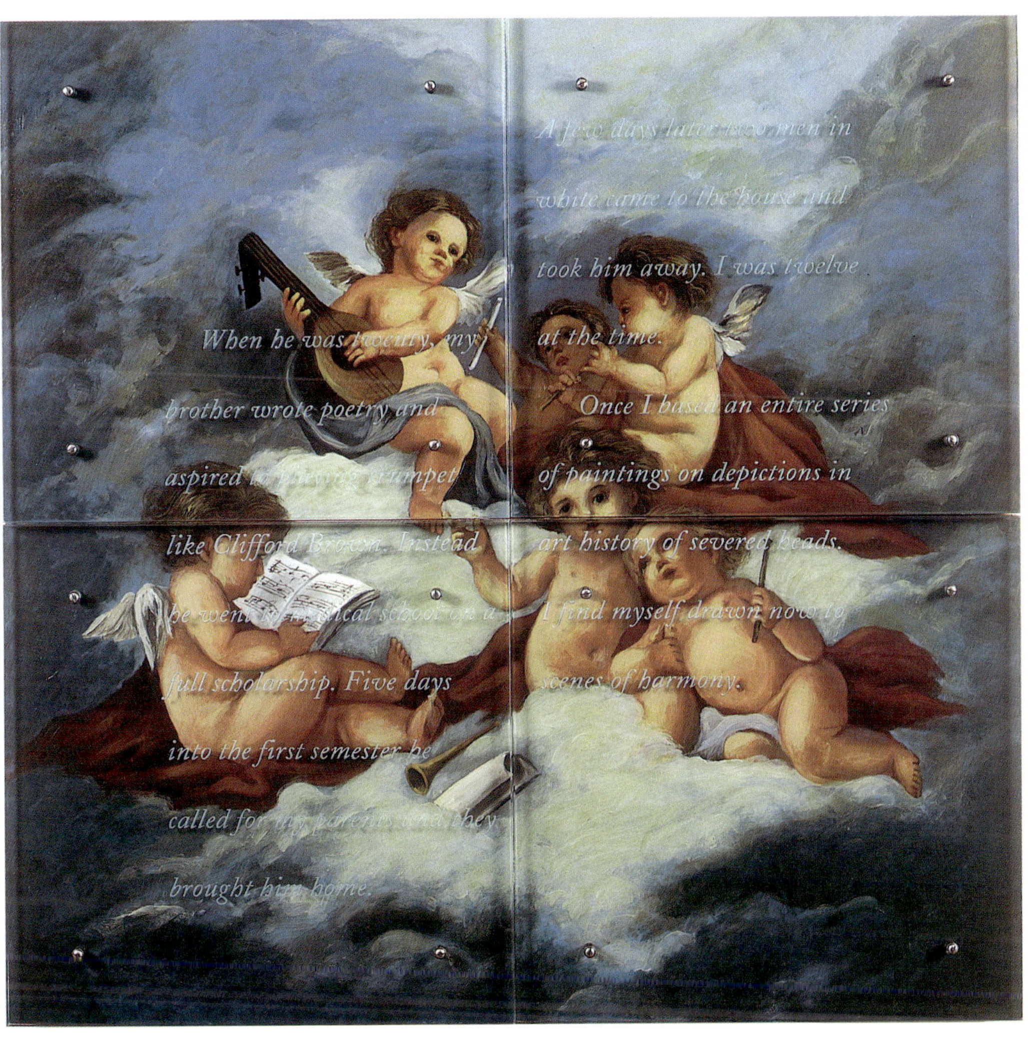

When he was twenty, my brother wrote poetry and aspired to playing trumpet like Clifford Brown. Instead he went to medical school on a full scholarship. Five days into the first semester he called for my parents and they brought him home. A few days later two men in white came to the house and took him away. I was twelve at the time. Once I based an entire series of paintings on depictions in art history of severed heads. I find myself drawn now to scenes of harmony.

PLATE 19

When he was twenty, 1997
Oil on wood, bolts, sandblasted glass
48" x 48" (4 panels)
Courtesy of Jack Shainman Gallery, New York

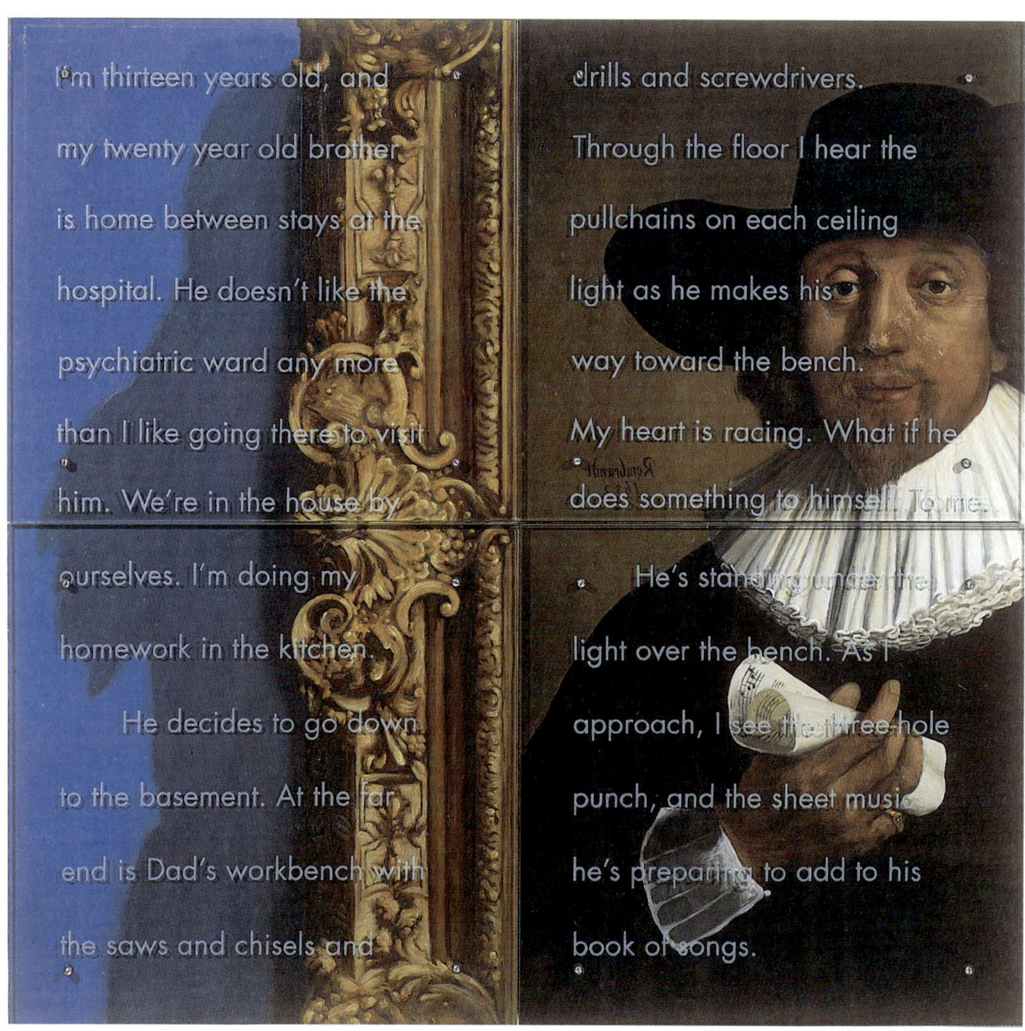

PLATE 20

I'm thirteen years old, 1997
Oil on wood, bolts, sandblasted glass
60" x 60" (4 panels)
Courtesy of Jack Shainman Gallery, New York

I'm thirteen years old, and my twenty year old brother is home between stays at the hospital. He doesn't like the psychiatric ward any more than I like going there to visit him. We're in the house by ourselves. I'm doing my homework in the kitchen. He decides to go down to the basement. At the far end is Dad's workbench with the saws and chisels and drills and screwdrivers. Through the floor I hear the pullchains on each ceiling light as he makes his way toward the bench. My heart is racing. What if he does something to himself. To me. He's standing under the light over the bench. As I approach, I see the three-hole punch, and the sheet music he's preparing to add to his book of songs.

"Both of 'em know something," the high school girl tells me, "like, say, she had an affair and he knows, but they never talked about it. Each one knows what the other is thinking, but they're not really talking and they're upset. They're holding something inside."

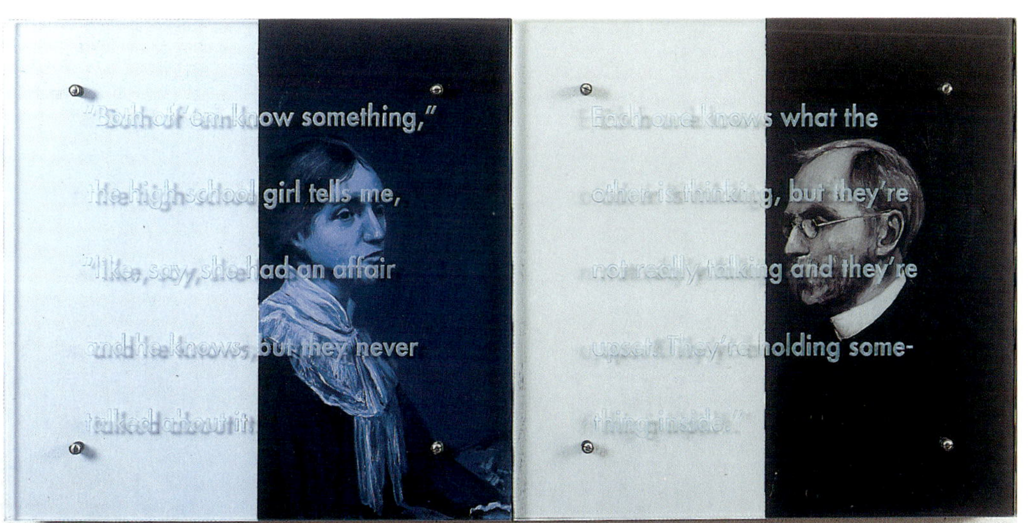

PLATE 21

"Both of 'em know something," 1997
Oil on wood, bolts, sandblasted glass
24" x 48" (2 panels)
Courtesy of Jack Shainman Gallery, New York

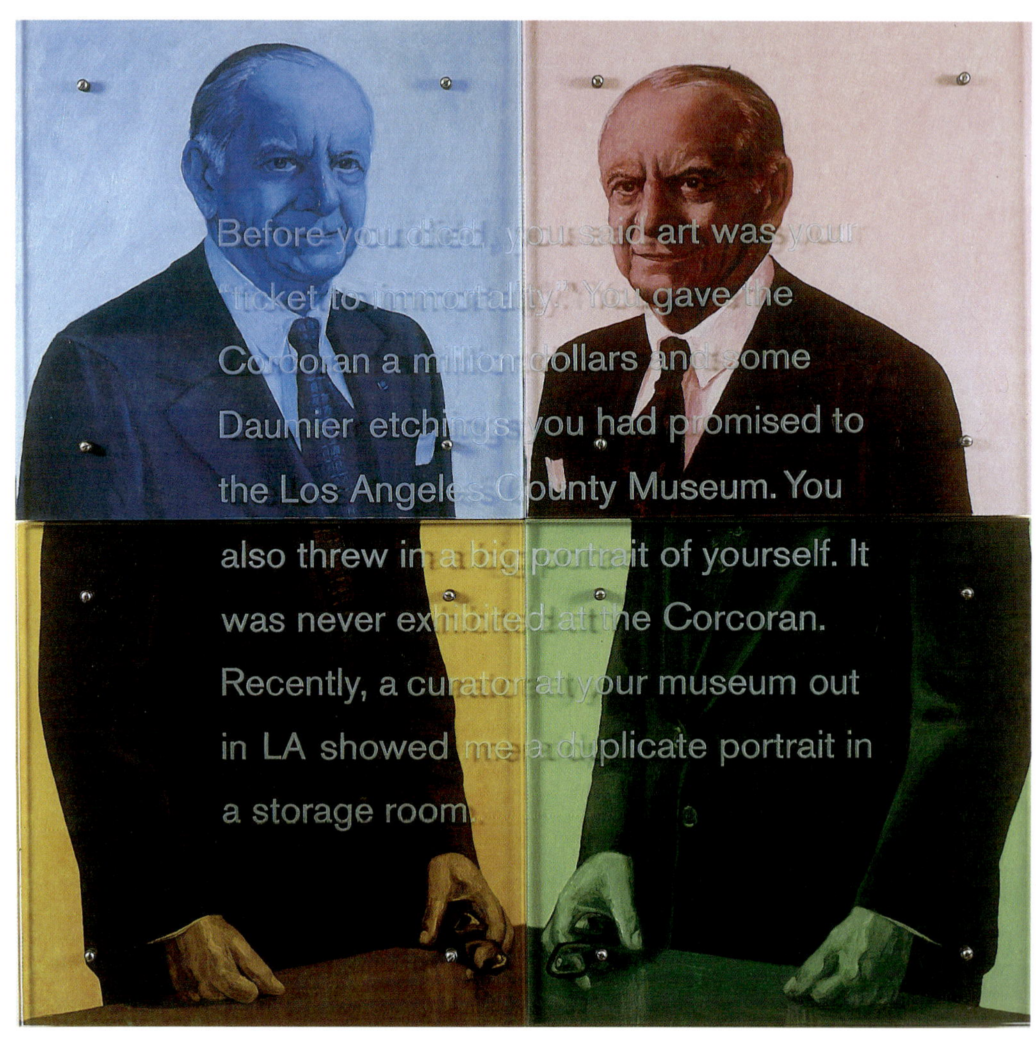

PLATE 22

Before you died, 1997
Oil on wood, bolts, sandblasted glass
48" x 48" (4 panels)
Courtesy of Jack Shainman Gallery, New York

Before you died, you said art was your "ticket to immortality." You gave the Corcoran a million dollars and some Daumier etchings you had promised to the Los Angeles County Museum. You also threw in a big portrait of yourself. It was never exhibited at the Corcoran. Recently, a curator at your museum out in LA showed me a duplicate portrait in a storage room.

I know there's lots of kids smoking and all, but that's setting a bad example. And for kids who haven't started smoking yet, that's not really sending a good message, you know? But art is art, and all art doesn't send a positive message. Akosua Tyus, age 14

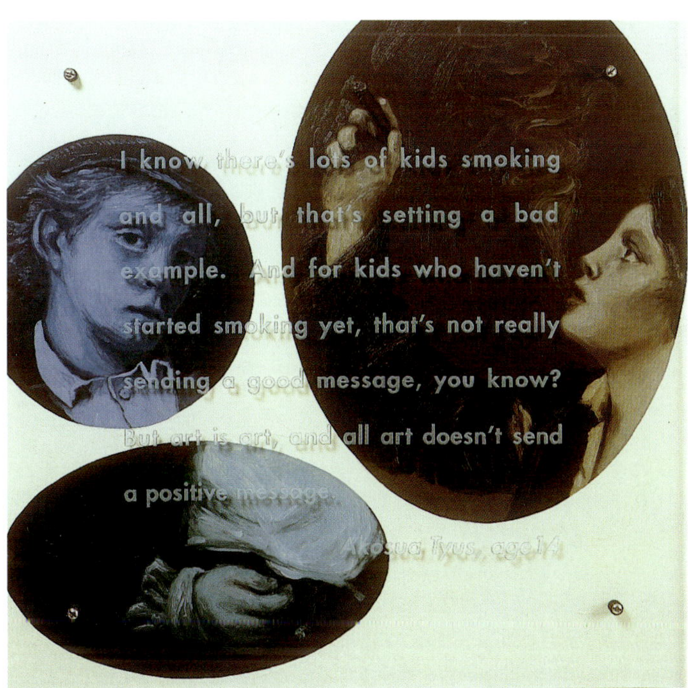

PLATE 23

I know there's lots of kids smoking, 1997
Oil on wood, bolts, sandblasted glass
30" x 30"
Courtesy of Jack Shainman Gallery, New York

Mollie Zwiebel says, "I'd buy a one-way ticket to Spain and send my big sister there forever."

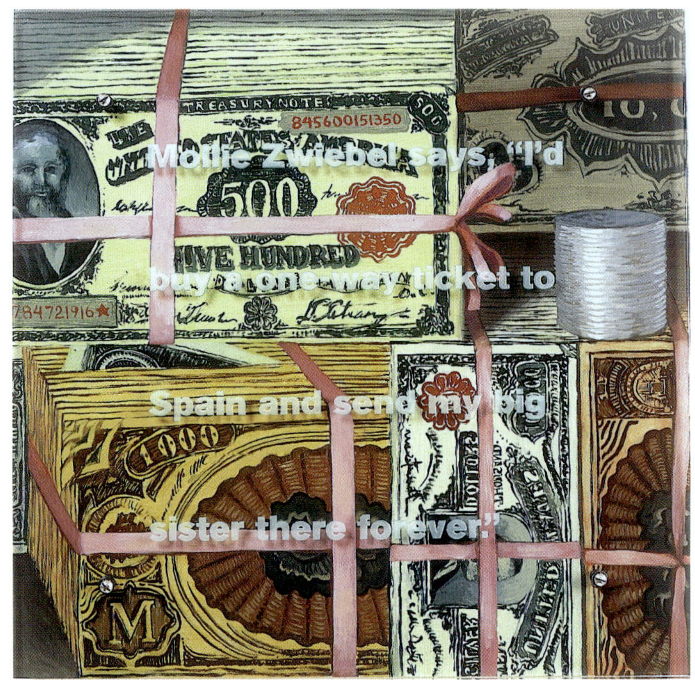

PLATE 24

Mollie Zwiebel says, 1997
Oil on wood, bolts, sandblasted glass
24" x 24"
Courtesy of Jack Shainman Gallery, New York

From Darnell Hester, a guard in the Corcoran: The gentleman seems like the kind of person I wouldn't want to know. I wouldn't trust him any further than I could see him. That's what I appreciate about the painting, the fact that it does arouse that type of emotion in me.

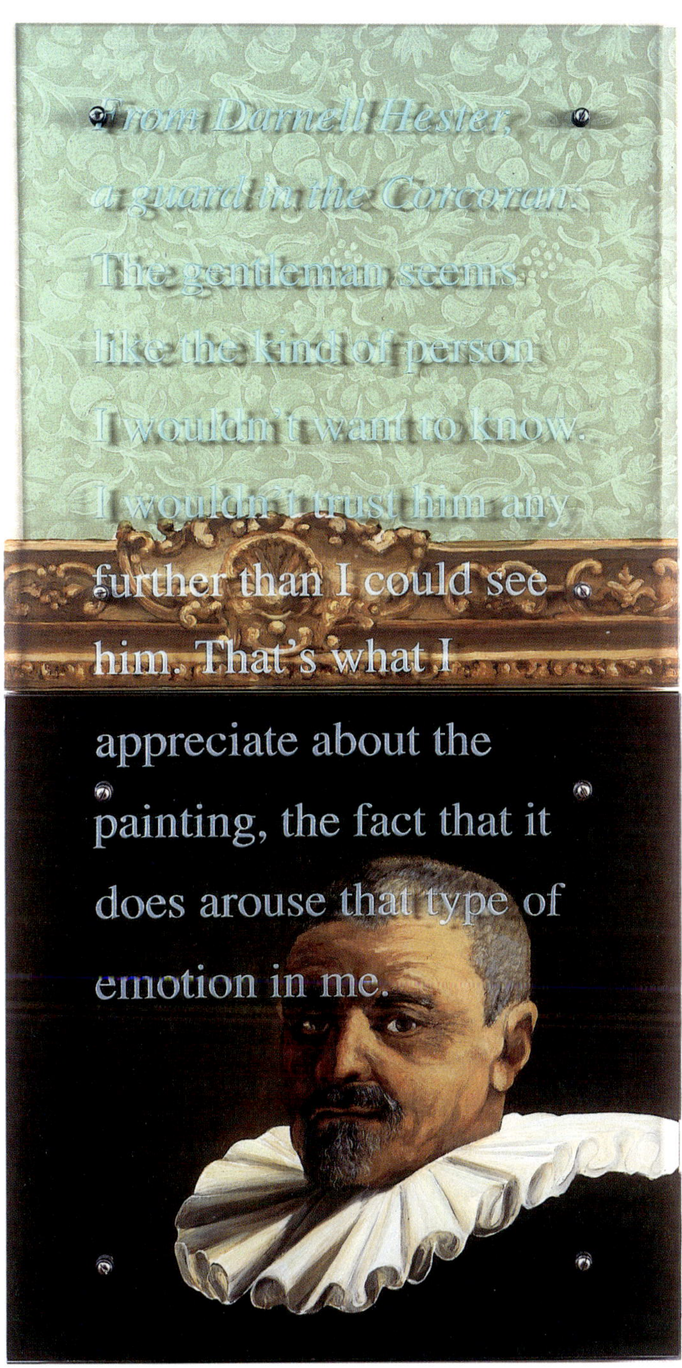

PLATE 25

From Darnell Hester, 1997
Oil on wood, bolts,
sandblasted glass
48" x 24" (2 panels)
Courtesy of Jack Shainman
Gallery, New York

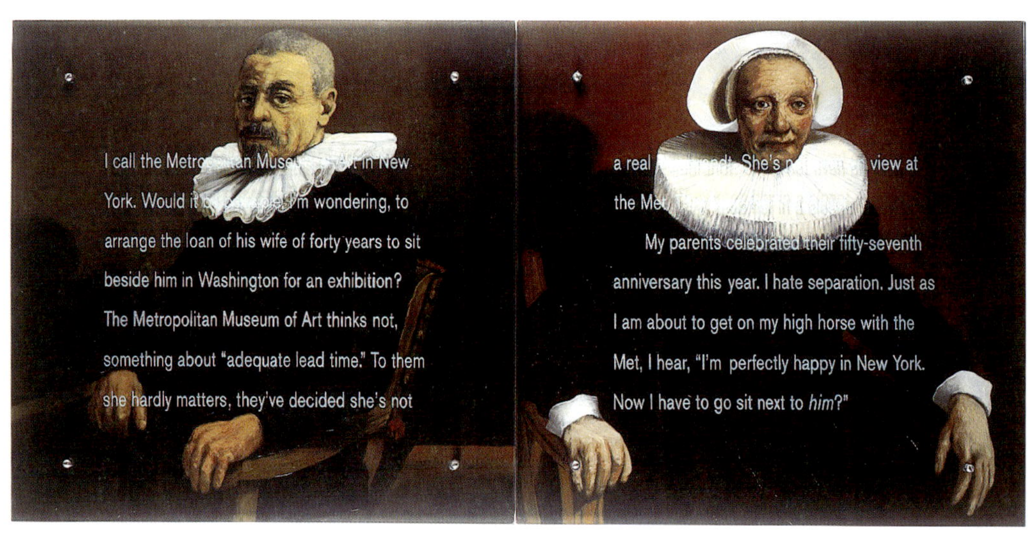

PLATE 26

I call the Metropolitan, 1997
Oil on wood, bolts, sandblasted glass
30" x 60" (2 panels)
Collection of Charles and Allison Garcia

I call the Metropolitan Museum of Art in New York. Would it be possible, I'm wondering, to arrange the loan of his wife of forty years to sit beside him in Washington for an exhibition? The Metropolitan Museum of Art thinks not; something about "adequate lead time." To them she hardly matters, they've decided she's not a real Rembrandt. She's not even on view at the Met. They keep her in a closet. My parents celebrated their fifty-seventh anniversary this year. I hate separation. Just as I am about to get on my high horse with the Met, I hear, "I'm perfectly happy in New York. Now I have to go sit next to him?"

My parents offer to help me buy a computer and scanner to work on my paintings. I get one with a 500 megabyte hard drive, which seems enormous. My studio is in the living room. So is the dining table, my desk, and a sitting area. I don't have much space to work. For a while, I just move my studio into cyberspace. Now the disk is full, and I really need a bigger room.

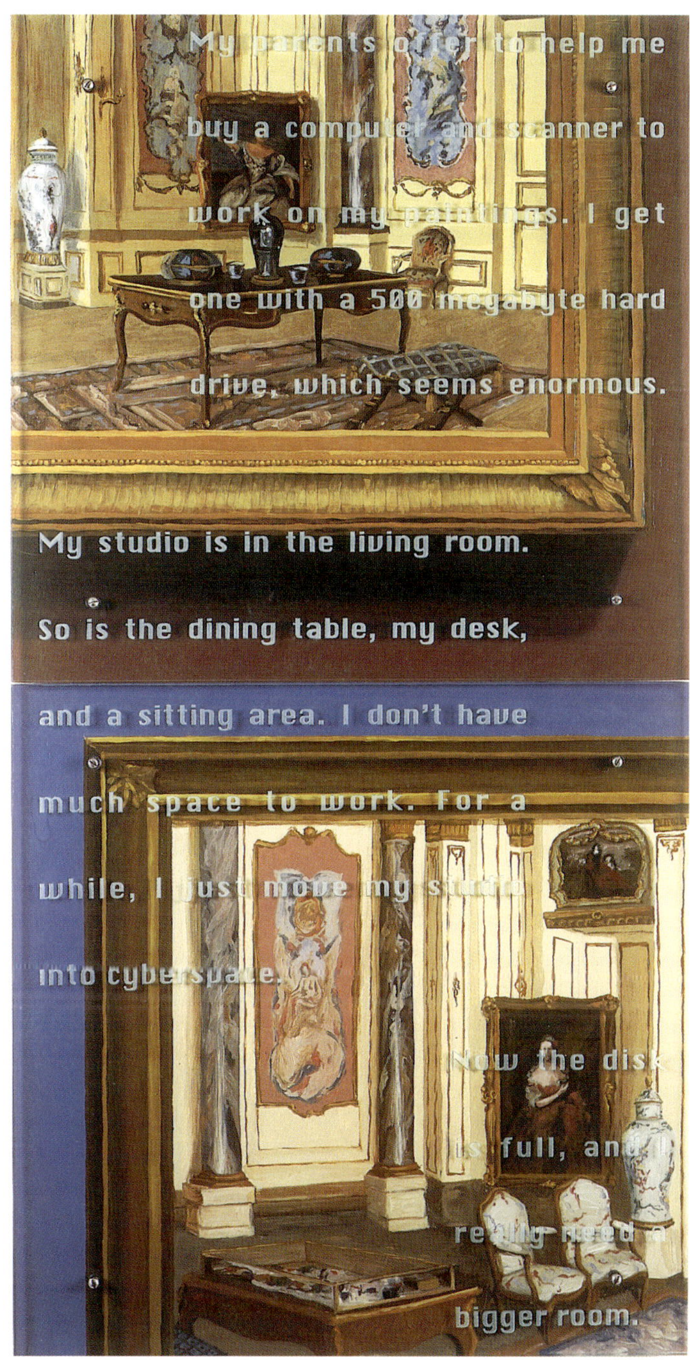

PLATE 27

My parents offer to help, 1997
Oil on wood, bolts,
sandblasted glass
60" x 30" (2 panels)
Courtesy of Jack Shainman
Gallery, New York

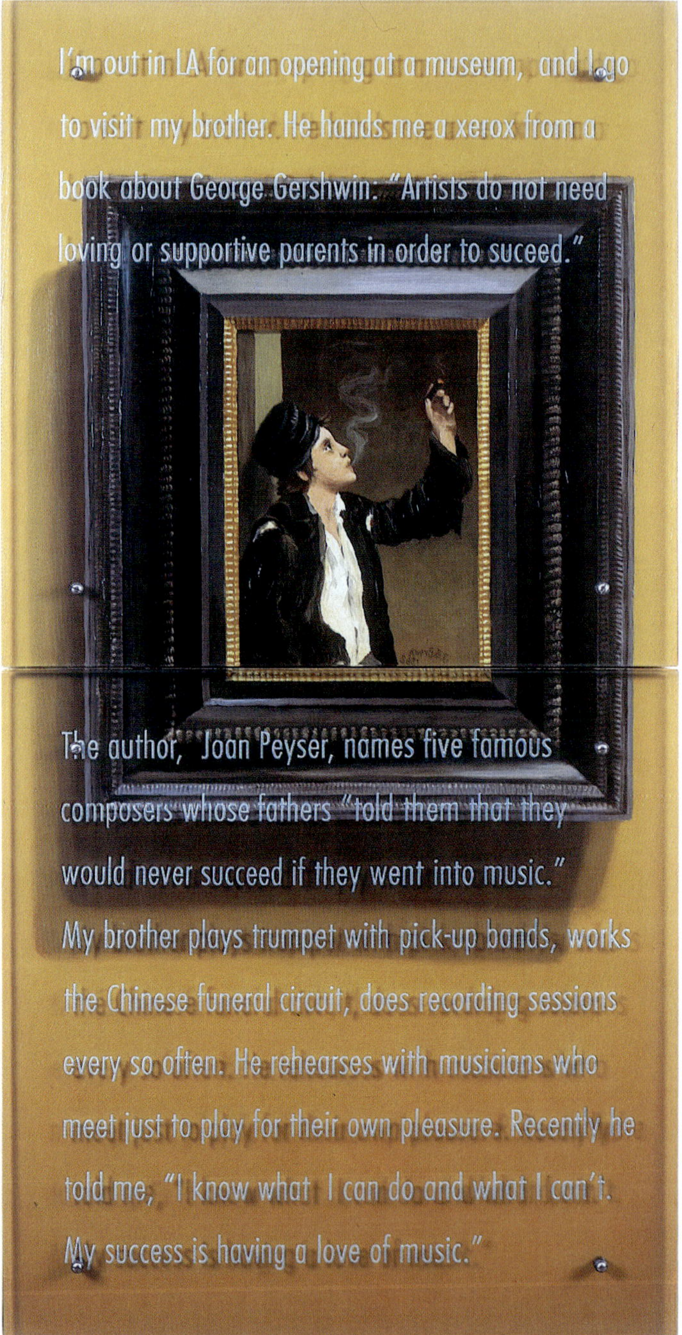

I'm out in LA for an opening at a museum, and I go to visit my brother. He hands me a xerox from a book about George Gershwin: "Artists do not need loving or supportive parents in order to succeed." The author, Joan Peyser, names five famous composers whose fathers "told them that they would never succeed if they went into music." My brother plays trumpet with pick-up bands, works the Chinese funeral circuit, does recording sessions every so often. He rehearses with musicians who meet just to play for their own pleasure. Recently he told me, "I know what I can do and what I can't. My success is having a love of music."

PLATE 28

I'm out in LA, 1997
Oil on wood, bolts,
sandblasted glass
60" x 30" (2 panels)
Courtesy of Jack Shainman
Gallery, New York

"I'd just look around and observe," Fatoumata Parrish, a guard at the Corcoran Gallery of Art, tells me. "I wouldn't sit in any of the chairs, because they look too pretty to sit in. No, I wouldn't touch anything," she says. "I'd just observe."

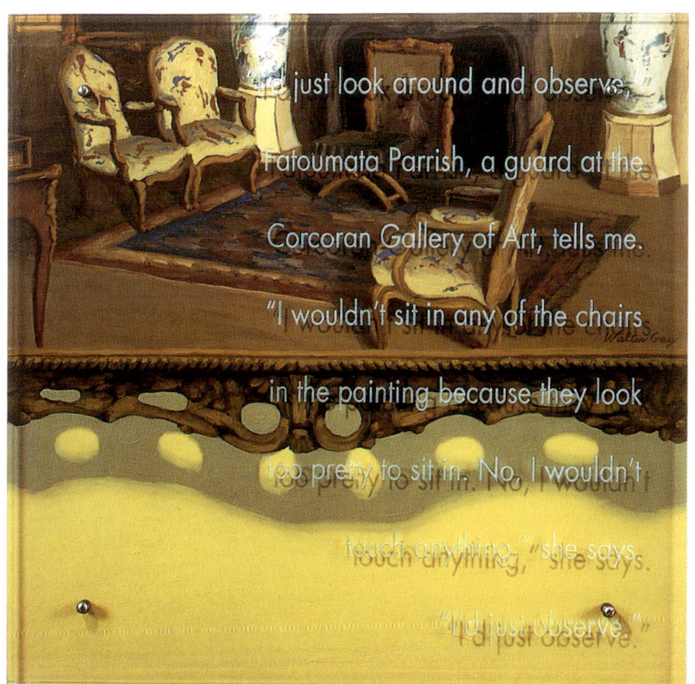

PLATE 29

"I'd just look around and observe," 1997
Oil on wood, bolts, sandblasted glass
30" x 30"
Private collection

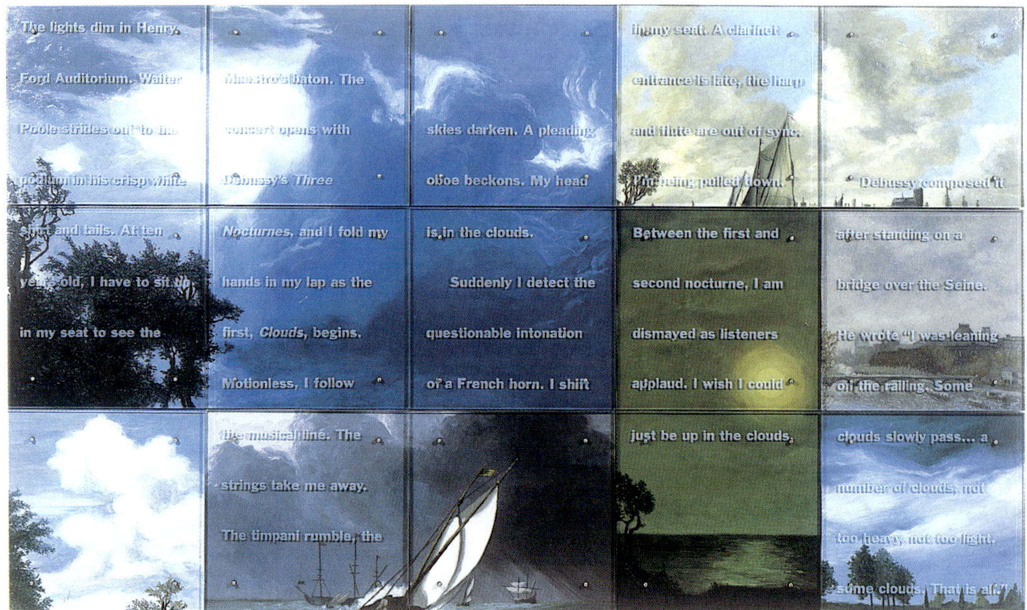

PLATE 30

The lights dim, 1997
Oil on wood, bolts, sandblasted glass
72" x 120" (15 panels)
Courtesy of Jack Shainman Gallery, New York

The lights dim in Henry Ford Auditorium. Walter Poole strides out to the podium in his crisp white shirt and tails. At ten years old, I have to sit up in my seat to see the Maestro's baton. The concert opens with Debussy's Three Nocturnes, *and I fold my hands in my lap as the first,* Clouds, *begins. Motionless, I follow the musical line. The strings take me away. The timpani rumble, the skies darken. A pleading oboe beckons. My head is in the clouds. Suddenly I detect the questionable intonation of a French horn. I shift in my seat. A clarinet entrance is late, the harp and flute are out of sync. I'm being pulled down. Between the first and second nocturne, I am dismayed as listeners applaud. I wish I could just be up in the clouds. Debussy composed it after standing on a bridge over the Seine. He wrote "I was leaning on the railing. Some clouds slowly pass… a number of clouds, not too heavy, not too light, some clouds. That is all."*

APTEKAR'S FAMILY ALBUM

Albert Boime

> *"I neologize Jewish and* goyish. *Dig: I'm Jewish. Ray Charles is Jewish. Eddie Cantor's* goyish. *B'Nai* [sic] *Brith is* goyish*; Hadassah, Jewish. Marine Corps—heavy* goyim...."
>
> — Lenny Bruce[1]

Ken Aptekar stands in relationship to the history of art as a troubled Jewish-American soul, and as a troublemaker who mentally can't stand still. He resembles both the wicked child of the Passover Seder ritual who asks all the pesky questions and the young secular Jewish rebel in Philip Roth's short story "Conversion of the Jews." Of course, "secular Jew" may be the ultimate oxymoron. Judaism has no closure until the Messiah comes, hence the Jewish condition can only be one of endless speculation and self-interrogation. When Aptekar began probing historical masterworks in 1992, he formulated polarities between Rembrandt and Raphael and Jewish-Gentile associations. Rembrandt's work, with its indications of family strife, contradiction, and anxiety, was posed against Raphael's transcendent images of harmony. Aptekar perceived here a contrast between Jewish questioning and Gentile lack of doubt: whereas Rembrandt asks questions, Raphael provides answers. For Aptekar answers are downers, while questions always give him some place to go; from his point of view, it is this seeking that leads to discovery and fulfillment.

This lack of closure constitutes a vital part of Judaism, and it also nurtures secular Jews; without the initial religious component, "secular Judaism" would be a contradiction in terms. The traditions of learning, of *Midrashim*, of commentary, of a political tradition with which many secular Jews identify, all derive from the religious tradition. A Jew is not constructed by either a text or a genetic code, but by a simple declaration of consent. Then the real struggle begins. A belief in a God who needs to be persuaded to do the right thing through argument or prayer amounts to the same thing as a rational social conscience—by choice, the Jew is an essentialist, whether secular or religious. Maintaining ethnic distinctiveness has become part of the multicultural project, but Jewish artists have until recently not represented themselves as Jews. Indeed, the Jewish presence in modern and avant-garde art has been profound but rarely singled out as such; generally speaking, it has been classified under a more amorphous national rubric. In the history of art, Jews as subjects were depicted mainly in biblical contexts, and as artists they hardly ever represented their community. Nevertheless, throughout this century, Jews have actively fought for egalitarian protection in areas such as civil rights, housing, and employment, and to this list Aptekar added the history of art.

Memory and historical continuity are crucial to a sense of Jewishness; when commemorat-

Adolf Ulrich Wertmüller
Portrait of Robert Lea, 1797

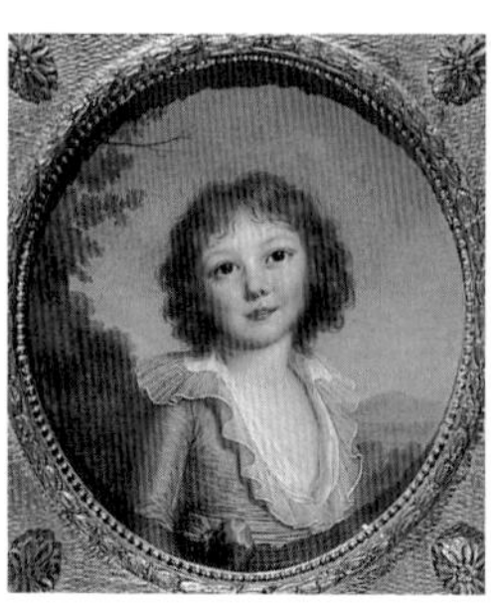

ing the Exodus of Egypt at Passover, the order of ritual is organized so that the participant sees him or herself as directly implicated in the narrative, as if among those liberated from bondage. This is what Aptekar does with his art, building on that shared Jewish tradition but universalizing it. In the process of reworking the Old Masters, Aptekar assimilates art history to his Jewish self and himself into that history. By allowing himself this unrestrained romp through the history of Old Master paintings, he gains the mobility he needs to free himself from the straitjacket of ethnic unconnectedness and reimagine an alternative tradition.

Aptekar's fantasies betray a comical impulse, but they implicate him as much as his audience. They are about his relatives, his ability to "pass" for Gentile. His parodies and reverential salutes to earlier masters diminish the aura of the original while affirming the artist's ethnicity—creating a sort of ethnic Dorian Gray. As Rembrandt assumes Jewish characteristics in Aptekar's recreations, so does the history of art and Aptekar's relationship to it. Parodic identification with a world-class celebrity by way of highlighting one's own depressed status is a favorite device of the Jewish humorist. After recalling the suicide of a Jewish kid that has the neighborhood in a turmoil, the protagonist of Philip Roth's *Portnoy's Complaint* raves on about suffocating Jewish mothers and blurts out that we [the sons] just "can't take any more!" Then, addressing his psychiatrist: "I have read Freud on Leonardo, Doctor, and pardon the hubris, but my fantasies exactly: this big, smothering bird beating frantic wings about my face and mouth *so that I cannot even get my breath.* What do we want, me and Ronald [the suicide] and Leonardo? *To be left alone*!" The implication is that Leonardo's mother was another Jewish mom.[2]

Aptekar's current exhibition, *Talking To Pictures,* applies Jewish self-irony to an unexpected site, the Corcoran Gallery of Art. William Wilson Corcoran, the museum's founder, was the quintessential representative of the power elite. White, Anglo-Saxon, Protestant, and male, Corcoran was a Southern sympathizer with racist and presumed anti-Semitic views reflective of those held by many in his social circle.[3] Instead of eliciting a dialogue between Old Masters, however, this time Aptekar pushes his process of democratizing the history of art by taking on the work of lesser-known artists in the museum's permanent collection. He dramatically engages with the collection on two mutually reinforcing levels: autobiographical and museological. Superimposing his autobiographical commentary over snippets of selected paintings in the form of texts etched

Yao You-Xin
Portrait of Dr. Armand Hammer, 1984

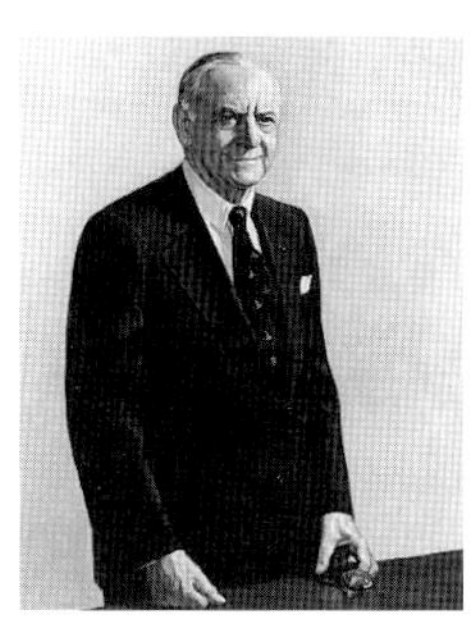

in glass, he also overlays messages concerning the sale, provenance, patronage, and subject matter of other pictures, carrying out a critique of the art market and institutional display mechanisms. These two strands of interest become interwoven as Aptekar worries about the subjectivities of the excluded "others" whose voices often appear as texts on his paintings.

One ingenious example of his museological critique is his mirror imaging of Yao You-Xin's portrait of Armand Hammer (donated to the Corcoran by Hammer himself) (PLATE 22). Hammer was a major benefactor of the Corcoran in the 1980s, using its proximity to the White House as a platform to ingratiate himself with the Washingtonian elite. Aptekar's text points out that this portrait was never exhibited, and that it was a replica of the portrait that once hung in the boardroom of Occidental Petroleum Corporation before being installed over the central staircase in what is now the Armand Hammer Museum and Cultural Center at the University of California-Los Angeles. Both the original and copy have now wound up in the storage room, remnants of a megalomaniac's reach for glory through the vehicle of the museum. Aptekar's text nails Hammer, reminding us that before he died, he declared that art was his "ticket to immortality."

Given Hammer's intensive involvement with the Corcoran, however, I was astonished that Aptekar did not juxtapose the oil magnate and art collector with the banker and museum founder. If there is a weakness in Aptekar's approach it is its lack of historical specificity. Granted that we give meaning to everything in creation, if the author-ventriloquist merely imparts his voice to any work in history, history can quickly lose its capacity to inform the present. In this case, Aptekar could have juxtaposed the Hammer portrait with the portrait (at least in reproduction) of Corcoran by Charles Loring Elliott. These two financial geniuses—one Protestant, the other Jewish—were born precisely a century apart (Corcoran in 1798, Hammer in 1898) and could easily have shared equal billing in a compare-and-contrast juxtaposition. Their respective credos are fascinating testimonies to their outsized egos. Here is Corcoran's dedicatory statement in the privately printed commemorative album presented to his grandchildren:

> *As a private individual, inspired by an appreciation of my relations to my fellow man, I have, from early youth to old age, endeavored to be just to all, and generous to the deserving. Blessed by kind Providence with large possessions more than commonly fall to the lot of man, I have regarded them as a sacred trust for the benefit of knowledge, truth, and charity. My reward has*

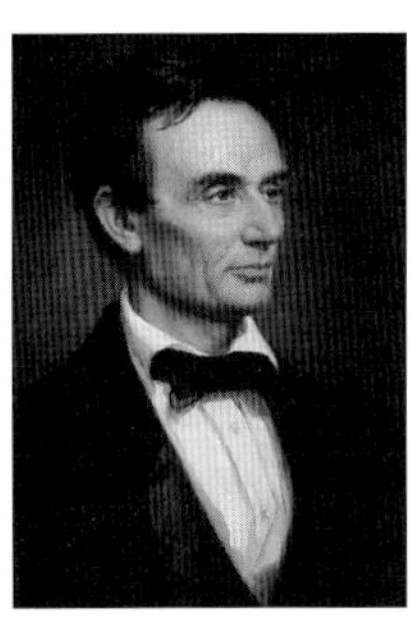

George Peter Alexander Healy
Abraham Lincoln, 1860

been an approving conscience, and the gratifying appreciation of many good and great men.[4]

And this is Hammer's autobiographical self-congratulation:

> *As a child, I composed a personal creed, which I would repeat to myself at bedtime.... I asked God, then, that I might be given the strength to help deserving people as much as I was able. I have never prayed for power or fame or riches, though I have enjoyed them all in abundance. I hope that I have never been greedy. All my life I have given away a large part of my fortune, more money than I could ever count.... I have tried to accomplish something of lasting benefit to the world; to add what I can to the riches of the planet and share with all the people the beauty and delight of life.*[5]

Both of these powerful and driven individuals assume the same sanctimonious air in justifying their loot, hoping to bury their complicated, corrupted pasts and buy for their posterity the myth of self-sacrifice and benevolence. It is clear both thought of themselves as embodiments of the American Dream: both were experts at self-promotion, and both avidly sought wealth at an early age. Corcoran built his fortune on Mexican war finance and the business of his pro-slavery constituents; at one time before the Civil War, he was the largest landowner in the District of Columbia. Hammer made his fortune in pharmaceuticals, selling an alcoholic-based ginger tincture during Prohibition. In Soviet Russia, he acted as intermediary for the sale of Czarist art treasures from aristocratic collections to American collectors and museums through his Gallery L'Ermitage in New York City. Neither Corcoran nor Hammer were connoisseurs of art, but both were skilled at first amassing and then exploiting art collections to promote their public image. Corcoran created his gallery dedicated to the "American Genius" to promote his status as a power broker in the nation's capital. He collected portraits of all the presidents and many famous statesmen, including a series of presidential portraits by George Peter Alexander Healy, one of which Aptekar has included in this exhibition. Over a century later, Hammer staged a highly publicized pre-inaugural party at the Corcoran Gallery of Art in honor of president-elect Reagan, exhibiting the Codex Hammer in order "to cultivate some of the richest and most powerful members of Washington society."[6]

What brings us back to Aptekar's exhibition is the surprising fact that when William Wilson Corcoran wanted niche statues for the exterior of the original Corcoran Gallery of Art (now the

Renwick Gallery), he commissioned Moses Ezekiel, a Jew caught up in the issue of Jewish identity in art production. This was the major commission of Ezekiel's career, and he presumably won it as much on the basis of the Southern sympathies he shared with his employer as for his talent. Ezekiel fought for the Confederate cause, and survived. By the close of the nineteenth century, when a Jewish national identity was beginning to be conceptualized, Ezekiel ridiculed the idea of the possibility of a distinctive Jewish art:

> *I must acknowledge that the tendency of the Israelites to stamp everything they undertake with such an emphasis is not sympathetic to my tastes. Artists belong to no country and to no sect....Everybody who knows me knows that I am a Jew—I never wanted it otherwise. But I would prefer as an artist to gain first a name and reputation upon an equal footing with all others in art circles. I do not wish to be stamped with the title of "Jewish sculptor."*[7]

Unlike Ezekiel, Aptekar wholeheartedly embraces his Jewishness as fundamental to his visual practice. Aptekar used three sources for his texts—historical information about the Corcoran and its collection, comments on the collection by people who participated in focus groups, and his own response to the works. These are juxtaposed with the artist's autobiographical recollections, creating a family album replete with all the secrets and lies associated with any carefully preserved, highly selective memory. Aptekar personalizes the museum's artifacts to discuss his complex relationships with both his creative immediate family and the larger art world. "Confessing" his family secret, he also establishes an arresting dialogue with artists of the past. The thematic core of *Talking To Pictures* is Aptekar's relationship with his brilliant brother, Stuart. Ken worries that he has usurped his brother's destined place in the world, and the exhibition's context provides him with the first opportunity to openly explore his conflicted feelings about his brother (PLATES 13, 14, 19, 20, 28).

Aptekar's parents were themselves skilled artists—his mother was a painter and art instructor, his father a musician and music teacher. They knew the insecurity of a life exclusively devoted to art practice, but they clearly handed down to their children artistic desires. However, while the parents trained their children artistically, they preferred them to practice as amateurs. Stuart's ambition was to write poetry and play trumpet in a jazz ensemble, but he was encouraged to conform with the stereotypical Jewish dream of "my son, the doctor." Stuart attended medical school at the University of Michigan on a full scholarship, but suffered a nervous breakdown five days after his arrival. He then spent several years in and out of hospitals.

Stuart suffered from being thwarted in his life's pursuit, and this suffering pointed up the contradictory nature of the American Dream in the postwar period. The gifted Stuart had been Ken's role model, but after his brother's breakdown, Ken could no longer recognize him as the handsome, talented student he had idolized. The trauma of this event was devastating to both, and left lasting repercussions. Stuart's fall from grace reduced his influence from role model to haunting specter, and some projection of this ghostliness can be seen in Ken's subsequent desire to first expunge and then explore his own historical memory. Ken's anxieties about ethnic erasure may very well have originated out of guilt over the possible disappearance of his fraternal "Other."

Aptekar's rollercoaster ride with his brother can be seen in his recuperation of Old Master portraits, specifically in the images of Rembrandt, whom he embraces as another sort of "brother." Aptekar seeks no father figure among Old Master forebears; rather, it is a "brother figure" to whom he appeals for dialogue. When Aptekar appropriates Old Master art, he plays off Stuart's brilliance; in this sense, his brother remains his imaginative enabler. Aptekar literally fraternizes with the Old Masters, questioning their authority, absorbing their talent, and entering into dialogue with them for the sake of affirming his own identity. In this sense, there never has been a disruption in the exchange between the two brothers. Hence, Aptekar's self-effacing approach to his art; it's not about Ken only, but also, by engaging history, about reaching out to Stuart and to Stuart's surrogates beyond time and space.

Ken and Stuart's shell-shocked parents, however, had, from the start, acted out of survivalist rather than materialist or authoritarian motives. Historically, Detroit has been a city rife with racial tension between whites and blacks in the automotive industry. There was also plenty of anti-Semitism to go around: Henry Ford's *Dearborn Independent* spewed its anti-Jewish venom in the 1920s, and in the next decade Father Coughlin of Detroit launched his virulent radio diatribes about the international Jewish conspiracy. But despite the general optimism of American Jews in the 1960s, Aptekar's family was taking no chances. A cautious mentality pervaded their strategic moves in the raising of their children—art is fine as a hobby but not as a full-time profession. Perhaps the main source of Ken's guilt has stemmed from the knowledge that Stuart, by

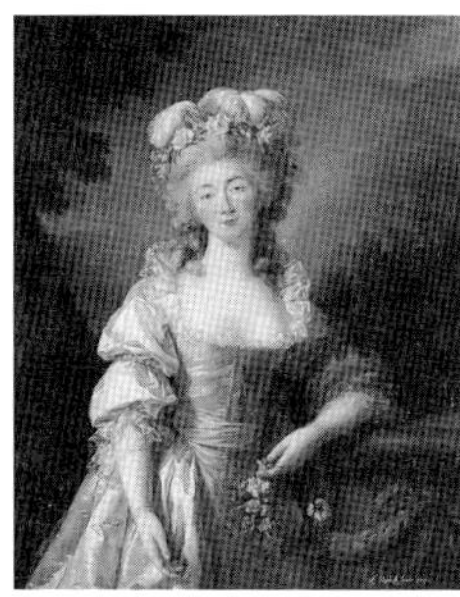

Elisabeth Vigée-Lebrun
Portrait of Madame du Barry, 1782

shouldering the burden of his parents' expectations, allowed Ken an escape hatch into the rarefied air of artistic ambition. Ken profited from Stuart's trauma, as his parents perhaps allowed him more space to nurture his painterly aptitude. Because of Stuart's experience, Ken was able to make his professional decision without the threat of parental interference.

Aptekar's work if anything is concrete, particular, and figurative. Modern in its politicized program, it is postmodern in its interrogation of the codes of art and art history. The opening work of *Talking To Pictures* depicts an empty frame, jauntily seen at an angle, floating on a wall. The text incorporates a statement by one of the museum's curators referring to the "ghosts in the collection" (PLATE 1). Through this reference, Aptekar demonstrates how the dubious practice of deaccessioning works for sale at auction to finance the purchase of other works is based on a slippery premise—one dominated by the subjective tastes of the living, who, through the act of deaccessioning, have rejected the legacy of their predecessors. The other myth that Aptekar examines is the notion of the Old Master signature: do we appreciate works because they are commercially valuable or because of their aesthetic appeal? Aptekar's running dialogue with the pictures of lesser-known artists, reinforced by his textual overlays, shows how one can come to love an image for its own sake.

Aptekar then fills the frame with Frederick Hendrick Kaemmerer's *The Beach at Scheveningen, Holland* (exhibited at the Paris Salon of 1874). Kaemmerer was initially a disciple of Gérôme; later he was seduced by the Impressionists' approach to light. In 1988 Corcoran contracted with Sotheby's to auction the painting, which sold for more than a million dollars. Aptekar uses Kaemmerer's image of the fashionable Dutch resort to recall his family outings to East Tawas on Lake Huron, and the comfort of being with parents and older siblings who love him (PLATE 2). But he notes a difference—as the lone redhead he has to cover up as protection from the sun. Even in the most escapist moments, he was aware of being different.

Citing another work, he uses the image of the famous French painter Elisabeth Vigée-Lebrun's fashionably dressed woman to evoke the immigrant experiences of his maternal grandmother, a talented and intelligent woman thwarted in her natural proclivities by the immigrants' struggle for economic survival (PLATE 5). She made his mother's clothes, and the mother recalls in Yiddish-accented English that, "A couturière your grandma could've been." The artist concludes,

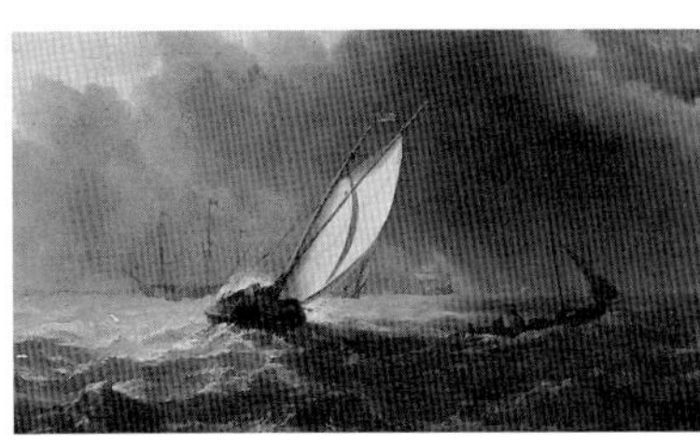

Willem Van de Velde the Younger
Before the Storm, c. 1700

"I escaped when I became an artist"—thus recognizing his links with his maternal ancestors and the French artistic tradition represented by one of its gifted females with whom he shares the singular opportunity to realize his full potential. Aptekar's humor takes off in his representation of Willem Van de Velde's seascape, *Before the Storm*. Here he intentionally reverses the image of the sailboat: reducing the palette to only red and black, Aptekar remembers his father teaching him how to use the darkroom facilities, using the enlarger properly "so the picture won't come out backwards. It's all up to me how big to make my pictures. Often I am all alone in the dark while I'm developing" (PLATE 8). Here Aptekar puns on the idea of image making and maturation, giving his male parent credit for stimulating his interest in imagery and affording him the chance to grow in solitude, to nurture his ideas without the pressure or interference that affected his older brother.

Aptekar's inspired vision even extends to decorated items of handicraft, in one case ingeniously incorporating an image from the museum's eighteenth-century harpsichord to frankly address the issue of his brother's breakdown. Against the instrument's rococo representations of cherubs playing music, he recalls that when he was twenty his brother aspired to write poetry and play the trumpet like Clifford Brown, whose album *Study in Brown* profoundly influenced jazz improvisation during the 1960s and 1970s. But instead Stuart went to medical school and suffered a breakdown. Fusing art and music into image and text to establish his family's precedents is perhaps his way of unifying the fragmented body, healing the scars of the past, and imagining the possibility of another plane of historical existence. Aptekar returns to one of his favorite sources (albeit one that is acknowledged to be merely "Rembrandt-ish" rather than a sure thing by the Rembrandt experts) for a moving recollection of being alone in the house with his brother between hospital stays. The subject of *I'm thirteen years old* has a curiously anxious look, appearing both skeptical and disturbed. In the text, the artist worries that his brother, who has just descended into the basement and is moving in the direction of their father's workbench with its myriad of tools, might harm himself. He hears the pull chains on each ceiling light leading to the workbench; the artist rushes downstairs to discover his brother with a "three-hole punch, and the sheet music he's preparing to add to his book of songs."

Aptekar also takes off on Henri Regnault's *Head of a Moor*, probably painted in 1870 when

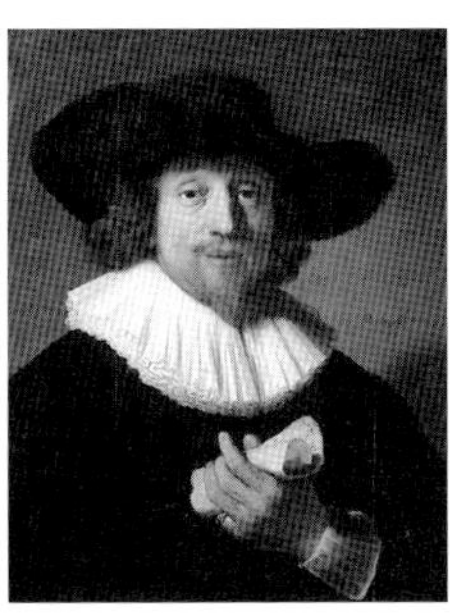

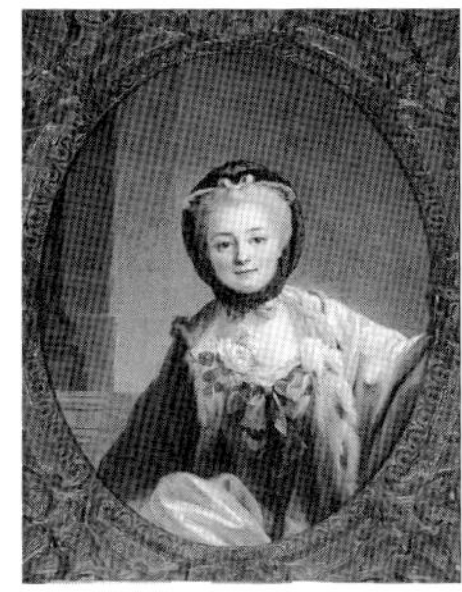

Circle of Rembrandt Van Rijn
Man with Sheet of Music, c. 1630

François-Hubert Drouais, *Portrait of Madame François-Hubert Drouais,* 1750

the French artist was residing in Tangier. Before returning to Paris, Regnault wrote, "I want to revive the true Moors, rich and grand, terrible and voluptuous at the same time, those that one could only see in the past."[8] The energetic and impulsive twist of the head could be a black version of Regnault himself, with his full head of curly hair, wild beard, and exuberant personality. Aptekar also projects onto the wood panels white traits of identification with Detroit's African-American community, now the majority in the central city. The inscribed text refers to the destitution of his brother after an automobile accident, when he lost his license, and Ken chauffeured him to bars in Detroit "where whites didn't go. I tried to be cool, sitting down in a booth with my ginger ale. My brother unzipped his gig bag, raised his trumpet, and sat in with the best of the be-bop bands" (PLATE 14). Here on the margins of middle-class white society, Stuart felt at home with another set of brothers.

Aptekar uses François-Hubert Drouais' *Madame François-Hubert Drouais,* another eighteenth-century woman whose bonnet reminds him of a babushka and he muses on another childhood scene in which he recalls practicing the piano, with his father listening attentively (PLATE 17). "Later my Russian grandmother is sitting on the couch. I'm playing *Oyfn Pripetshik* for her. I see her lips moving to the Yiddish lyrics she learned in a village near Minsk sixty years ago. My grandmother died in 1982. I don't play piano much anymore." The assumption here is that it was the saintly grandmother's warmth and affection that inspired him intellectually as well as the father's discipline. He associates her with the Russian folk song by Mark Warschavsky, *In the Little Stove*, that conveys the image of the East European schoolboys at *kheder* (Hebrew school), huddled around a wood stove learning the Hebrew alphabet, the *alefbeis*, from their *rebbe*. It is this affection that he detects in Drouais' portrait of another era, enabling him to tap into feelings for his grandmother and bridge the gap between loss and remembrance.

Aptekar closes his dialogue with a series of cloud vignettes derived from an international mélange that includes American painters Albert Bierstadt and Ralph Albert Blakelock, the Dutch landscapist Jan Van Goyen, and French artists Charles-François Daubigny and Camille Pissarro (PLATE 30). These set him to dreaming about the time his family took him to a concert conducted by Valter Poole in the Henry Ford Auditorium. The concert opens with Debussy's *Three Nocturnes*, the first of which is "Clouds." In his memory Aptekar follows the instrumentation

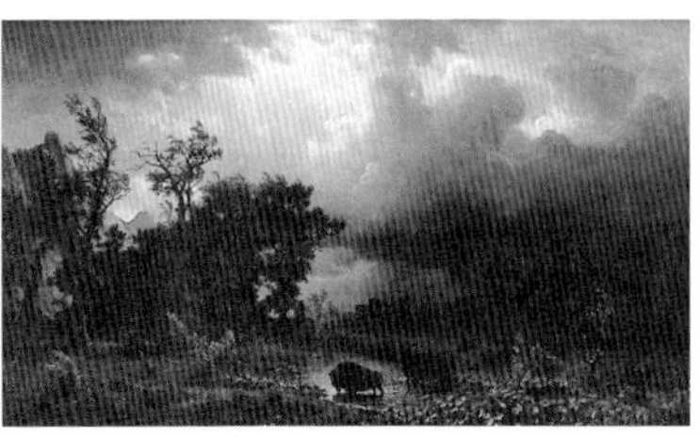

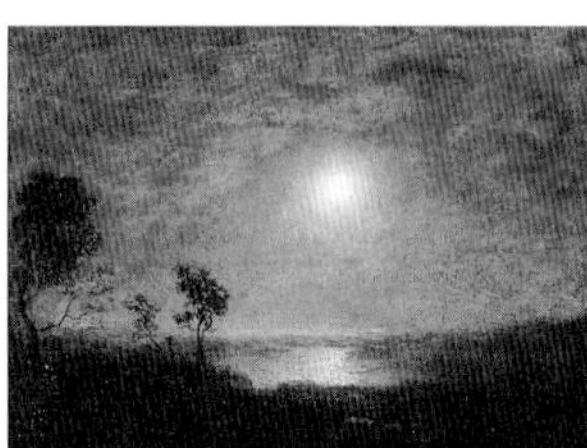

Albert Bierstadt,
The Buffalo Trail: The Impending Storm, 1869

Ralph Albert Blakelock,
Moonlight, c. 1890

carefully, gets carried away by the strings and floats "in the clouds." Then things go wrong: he "detect(s) the questionable intonation of a French horn....A clarinet entrance is late, the harp and flute are out of sync." With this mishmash, Aptekar feels himself being "pulled down," and wants to overcome gravity and return to the clouds. He ends his text with the historical recollection that Debussy composed the work standing on a bridge over the Seine watching clouds slowly pass, and appropriately the image that coincides with this text is Pissarro's Parisian landscape. It is also fitting that Aptekar closes this series with the work of a Jewish Impressionist.

Aptekar's pictorial dialogue with the collection begins talking about ghosts in the museum closet and ends discussing ghosts in the family closet. Spotlighting the museum's practice of canceling the standing of both works of art and their makers, he draws an analogy between the museum's elimination of a piece of its history and art history's practice of relegating ethnic minorities to the margins. His dialogue terminates with the tangible continuity of Jewish creativity in the face of life's perils. Above all, he acknowledges his family as the complicated source of his creative energies—making the unmistakable connection between their absorption in music and the kind of work he does. Thus Aptekar closes the family album with a record of the loving synthesis of art and music that constituted the driving force of his family's lives. In the end, I believe, his success—and fame—may best be understood as a "family affair."

Much of this commentary was based on a series of interviews with the artist in Los Angeles on January 27 and January 29, 1997. I am grateful to him for generously sharing his thoughts with me, and to Myra Boime for her constructive reading of my manuscript.

1. John Cohen, ed., *The Essential Lenny Bruce* (New York: Ballantine, 1967), 41-42 (original emphasis).
2. Philip Roth, *Portnoy's Complaint* (New York: Random House, 1969), 121 (original emphasis).
3. Davira Spiro Taragin, "William Wilson Corcoran, 1798-1888," in the *Corcoran Gallery of Art* (Washington, DC, 1976), 5-9; Alan Wallach, "On the Problem of Forming a National Art Collection in the United States: William Wilson Cororan's Failed National Gallery," in *The Formations of National Collections of Art and Archaeology*, ed. Gwendolyn Wright, (National Gallery of Art, Washington, DC, 1996), 113-23.
4. William Wilson Corcoran, *A Grandfather's Legacy; Containing a Sketch of His Life...*(Washington, DC, 1879), dedicatory page.
5. Armand Hammer with Neil Lynon, *Hammer* (New York, 1987), 13-14.
6. Carl Blumay with Henry Edwards, *The Dark Side of Power: the Real Armand Hammer* (New York: Simon & Schuster, 1992), 318.
7. Moses Jacob Ezekiel, *Memoirs from the Baths of Diocletian*, eds. Joseph Gutmann and Stanley F. Chyet, (Detroit: Wayne State University Press, 1975), 21.
8. A. Duparc, *Correspondance de Henri Regnault* (Paris: Bibliothèque Charpentier, 1873), 342.

EDUCATION

1975 MFA, Pratt Institute, Brooklyn

1973 BFA, University of Michigan, Ann Arbor

SELECTED AWARDS AND FELLOWSHIPS

1995 National Endowment for the Arts

1992 Rockefeller Foundation Artist Residency
Ucross Foundation

1991, 94 Djerassi Foundation

1989 Pollock–Krasner Foundation Award

1987 National Endowment for the Arts

SELECTED SOLO EXHIBITIONS

1997 "Ken Aptekar: Talking to Pictures," The Corcoran Gallery of Art, Washington, DC

1996 Jack Shainman Gallery, New York

1995 "Rembrandt Redux: The Paintings of Ken Aptekar," Palmer Museum of Art, Pennsylvania State University, University Park (traveled to Cummer Museum, Jacksonville, Florida)

1994 Jack Shainman Gallery, New York

1990 Margulies Taplin Gallery, North Miami

1989 Bess Cutler Gallery, New York

1984 Sid Deutsch Gallery, New York

1983 "On View," New Museum of Contemporary Art, New York

1980 Art Galaxy, New York

1979 Art Latitude, New York

SELECTED GROUP EXHIBITIONS

1996 "Narcissism: Artists Reflect Themselves," California Center for the Arts Museum, Escondido
"Masculine Measures," Kohler Arts Center, Sheboygan, Wisconsin
"Too Jewish?: Challenging Traditional Identities," The Jewish Museum, New York (Traveled to the Jewish Museum, San Francisco; Armand Hammer Museum, Los Angeles; The Contemporary, Baltimore; National Museum of American Jewish History, Philadelphia) [catalogue]

1995 "Art Without Borders," Ecole du Versant, Larouche, Quebec
"And the Verdict is… ," Jack Shainman Gallery, New York
"Going for Baroque," Walters Art Gallery, Baltimore (organized jointly with Lisa Corrin of The Contemporary, Baltimore) [catalogue]
"Human/Nature," New Museum of Contemporary Art, New York

1994 "New Old Masters," Center for the Arts at Yerba Buena Gardens, San Francisco [catalogue]
"Bad Girls West," Wight Art Gallery at UCLA, Los Angeles

1993 "43rd Biennial Exhibition of Contemporary American Painting," The Corcoran Gallery of Art, Washington, DC [catalogue]

	"The Purloined Image," Flint Institute of Arts, Flint, Michigan [catalogue]
1992	"Decoding Gender," School 33 Art Center, Baltimore
1991	"New Generation: New York," Carnegie Mellon University Art Museum, Pittsburgh [catalogue]
1990	"Post–Boys & Girls: Nine Painters, Artists Space, New York "June 4, 1989, China," Institute for Contemporary Art, P.S. 1 Museum, Long Island City, New York
1989	"Gender Fictions," State University of New York at Binghamton Art Museum "Serious Fun, Truthful Lies," Randolph Street Gallery, Chicago
1987	"The Other Man: Alternative Representations of Masculinity," New Museum of Contemporary Art, New York
1986	Art in General, New York

SELECTED BIBLIOGRAPHY

"Paintings That Get Personal." *The Forward*, 25 October, 1996, p. 8.

"The National Art Scene." *New York Times*, 5 January 1997, 17.

Aptekar, Ken. "Dear Rembrandt." *Art Journal* 54, no. 3 (Fall 1995), 12–13.

Atkins, Robert. "New This Week: Ken Aptekar." *Seven Days* (13 December 1989).

Baker, Kenneth. "Contemporary Painting Celebrated in DC." *San Francisco Chronicle*, 7 November 1993, 46–47.

Bal, Mieke. *Over Kunst, Literatuur en Filosofie: Liber Amicarum*. eds. H.J. Pott, V. Vasterling, R. van de Vall, and K. Vintges.

Edelman, Robert G. "The Figure Returns: 43rd Corcoran Biennial." *Art in America* 82 (March 1994), 38–41.

Grimes, Nancy. "Ken Aptekar at Jack Shainman." *Art in America* 82, no. 11 (November 1994), 130–31.

Hagen, Asmout. "Ken Aptekar klest ult Rembrandts hoedencollectie." *Kroniek van Het Rembrandthuis (Chronicle of the Rembrandt House)* no. 1 (1995), 29–35.

Henry, Gerrit. "Ken Aptekar at Bess Cutler." *Art in America* 78, no. 6 (June 1990), 180.

Hess, Elizabeth. "Yesterday's Children." *The Village Voice,* 4 December 1990.

Kanaff, Devorah. "Standing Out, Blending In, Knowing Oneself." *San Diego Union-Tribune*, 16 February 1997, E9.

Kimmel, Michael S. "Too Jewish? What Do You Mean By That? Izzet a Stereotype?...." *Westsider,* 11 April 1996.

Knight, Christopher. "Bad Girls: Feminism on Wry." *Los Angeles Times*, 8 February 1994.

McWilliams, Martha. "Go Figure." *Washington City Paper*, 12 November 1993, 43.

Miller, Donald. "Contemporary Shows Join With Rembrandt Etchings." *Pittsburgh Post Gazette*, 4 February 1995, C6.

Raynor, Vivien. "Bedrooms and Drawings." *New York Times*, 17 February 1991, 14.

Risatti, Howard. "43rd Corcoran Biennial." *Artforum* 32 no. 7 (March 1994), 92.

Roth, Charlene. "Bad Girls: Feminism on Wry." *Los Angeles Times*, 8 February 1994.

Saslow, James. "Rethinking Masculinity: Ken Aptekar." *The Advocate*, 22 May 1990, 54–55.

Shearing, Graham. "Remarkable Rembrandt: Three shows celebrate the artist." *Pittsburgh Tribune–Review*. 15 January 1995, E5.

Slid, Gerard. "Reframes and Refrains: Artists Rethink Art History." *Art Journal* 54, no. 3 (Fall 1995), 10–11.

Zimmer, William. "Kenneth Aptekar at Sid Deutsch." *Arts Magazine* 58, no. 9 (May 1984), 19.

FROM THE COLLECTION OF THE CORCORAN GALLERY OF ART

Bierstadt, Albert, *The Buffalo Trail: The Impending Storm*, 1869, Museum Purchase through the gift of Mr. and Mrs. Landsdell K. Christie

Blakelock, Ralph Albert, *Moonlight,* c. 1890, William A. Clark Collection

Brown, John George, *Allegro*, 1864; and *Penseroso*, 1865, Gift of William Wilson Corcoran

Chase, Harry, *The Harbor of York*, 1885, Gallery Fund

Circle of Rembrandt Van Rijn, *Man with Sheet of Music*, c. 1630, William A. Clark Collection

Circle of Rembrandt Van Rijn, *An Elderly Man in an Armchair*, c. 1630, William A. Clark Collection

Daubigny, Charles-François, *Landscape, Distant Village*, 1870–75, Bequest of George Lothrop Bradley and Helen McHenry Bradley

Dedeban, Jean Mari, *Harpsichord* (cupid groupings on the side), 1770, William A. Clark Collection

Drouais, François-Hubert, *Portrait of Madame François-Hubert Drouais*, 1750, William A. Clark Collection

Dubreuil, Victor, *Safe Money*, 1896, Museum Purchase through a gift from the heirs of George E. Lemon

Elliott, Charles Loring, *Thomas Loraine McKenney*, 1856, Bequest of James C. McGuire

Gay, Walter, *Salon in the Musée-Jacquemart André*, n.d., Museum Purchase through the gift of Orme Wilson

Healy, George Peter Alexander, *Abraham Lincoln*, 1860, Museum Purchase, Gallery Fund

Hobbema, Meyndert, *A Wooded Landscape with Figures*, c. 1663, William A. Clark Collection

Kaemmerer, Frederick Hendrick, *The Beach at Scheveningen, Holland*, 1874 (deaccessioned in 1988)

Pissarro, Camille, *The Louvre, Morning, Rainy Weather*, 1900, Edward C. and Mary Walker Collection

Regnault, Henri, *Head of a Moor*, 1870, Gift of Mr. R. Max Kauffmann

Richards, William Trost, *On the Coast of New England*, 1894, Gift of the heirs of George E. Lemon

Shirlaw, Walter, *Self-Portrait*, n.d., Gift of Miss Florence Heywood

Ulrich, Charles Frederick, *In the Land of Promise, Castle Garden*, 1884, William A. Clark Collection

Van Goyen, Jan, *View of Dordrecht (from the North)*, c. 1651, William A. Clark Collection

Van de Velde, Willem the Younger, *Before the Storm*, c. 1700, William A. Clark Collection

Vigée-Lebrun, Elisabeth, *Portrait of Madame Du Barry*, 1782, William A. Clark Collection

Wertmüller, Adolf Ulrich, *Portrait of Robert Lea*, 1797, Anonymous gift

Wiles, Irving Ramsey, *The Artist's Mother and Father*, 1889, William A. Clark Collection

Yewell, George Henry, *Portrait of a Boy*, 1867, Gift of Mr. and Mrs. Louis E. Schecter

You–Xin, Yao, *Portrait of Dr. Armand Hammer*, 1984, Gift of Dr. Armand Hammer

This book has been published in conjunction with
KEN APTEKAR: TALKING TO PICTURES
Organized by the Corcoran Gallery of Art, and serves as the catalogue for the exhibition.

THE CORCORAN GALLERY OF ART
500 Seventeenth Street NW
Washington DC 20006-4804
October 18 – February 15

This exhibition and book were made possible in part by the support of The President's Exhibition Fund, the FUNd at the Corcoran, Jarboe Printing Company, Inc., and Mr. and Mrs. Michael Abrams.

CURATOR: Terrie Sultan, Curator of Contemporary Art

ESSAYISTS: Mieke Bal, Albert Boime

PROJECT MANAGER: Paige Turner

EDITOR: Christopher French

LENDERS TO THE EXHIBITION

Ron and Anne Dees

Drs. Ernest and Louise De Salvo

Charles and Allison Garcia

Dr. Lucy Daniels Inman

Dr. Gail Postal

Jack Shainman Gallery, New York

Marcia Cohn Spiegel

Cynthia Stein

ARTIST'S ACKNOWLEDGEMENTS

Terrie Sultan and Paige Turner, Christina Segovia, Ron Dees, Marisa Keller, Linda Crocker Simmons, and John Lewis, the Corcoran Gallery of Art.

Ruth Adams, Ernst van Alfen, Lucille Aptekar and Gerald Leader, Stuart Aptekar, Richard Aptekar, Anne and Milton Aptekar, Robert Atkins, Dotty Attie, Mieke Bal, Carol Becker, Clare Bell, Albert Boime, Norman Bryson, Lisa Corrin, Dr. Sandra Hershberg, Joel Kostman, Lauren Lesko, Joan Rosenbaum, David Savran, Meryl Schwartz, Elizabeth Shepherd, Marcia Cohn Spiegel, Jorge Daniel Veneciano, Carrie Mae Weems. An extra special thanks to Eunice Lipton, Jack Shainman, Claude Simard, and Sarah Douglas of the Jack Shainman Gallery; Xing Li of New Time Art in Glass, New York, for his sandblasting; Simon Liu of Simon's Stretchers, Brooklyn, New York.

The artist and the Corcoran Gallery of Art thank the participants in the focus groups, including the teachers and students of Georgetown Day School, High School without Walls, and the Corcoran School of Art as well as the Corcoran guards who came in early to meet with the artist.

This catalogue was designed by Timothy B. Connor, the Corcoran Gallery of Art, Washington, DC, and typeset in Adobe Bembo. 2,000 copies were printed on Mead Signature and Glama Natural by Chroma Graphics, Inc., Largo MD.

Photography for PLATES 8, 20, 30 by D. James Dee.